Libraries
ReadLearnConnect

THIS BOOK IS PART OF ISLINGTON READS BOOKSWAP SCHEME

Please take this book and either return it to a Bookswap site or replace with one of your own books that you would like to share.

If you enjoy this book, why not join your local Islington Library and borrow more like it for free?

Find out about our FREE e-book, e-audio, newspaper and magazine apps, activities for pre-school children and other services we have to offer at www.islington.gov.uk/libraries

ISLINGTON
For a more equal future

ON YOUR MARKS, GET SET... GOLD!

TO GWEN,
"THERE'S A GOOD FILM ON TONIGHT..."
— S. A.

TO MY DEAR LITTLE CHAMPIONS,
JULIETTE ET BASILE
— A. C.

First published 2021 by Nosy Crow Ltd.
This edition published 2024 by Nosy Crow Ltd.
Wheat Wharf, 27a Shad Thames,
London, SE1 2XZ, UK

Nosy Crow Eireann Ltd.
44 Orchard Grove, Kenmare,
Co Kerry, V93 FY22, Ireland

www.nosycrow.com

ISBN 978 1 80513 072 7

Nosy Crow and associated logos are trademarks
and/or registered trademarks of Nosy Crow Ltd.

Text © Scott Allen 2021
Illustrations © Antoine Corbineau 2021

The right of Scott Allen to be identified as the author and Antoine Corbineau
to be identified as the illustrator of this work has been asserted.

A CIP catalogue record for this book is available from the British Library.

Printed in China following rigorous ethical sourcing standards.
Papers used by Nosy Crow are made from wood
grown in sustainable forests.

135798642

ON YOUR MARKS, GET SET... GOLD!

A FACT-FILLED, FUNNY GUIDE TO EVERY OLYMPIC SPORT

Written by
Scott Allen

nosy crow

Illustrated by
Antoine Corbineau

Contents

PUSHING THE LIMITS

MAKING A RACKET

Riding High

INTRODUCTION

Hello, and welcome to your ultimate fact-filled and funny guide to the Olympic and Paralympic Games. Every sport featured in the Paris 2024 Olympic Games will be covered in detail in this book - some sports might be totally new to you, others you have probably heard of before but never tried yourself, and a few you might even play already. All of the sports featured in this guide have one thing in common - the athletes involved with them all have a chance to win a coveted, shiny Olympic gold medal!

Most gold medal winners start their journey when they're still at school, and some athletes even start while they're in nappies! They face a roller coaster of emotion and physical torment, but top athletes stay strong, grit their teeth and battle for glory. Nobody wins an Olympic gold medal without putting in plenty of hard work, so training is essential and it comes in lots of different shapes and sizes. This guide might give you an extra edge against your rivals or make your dad angry that you've ruined his carpet. In the world of sport, everyone has to make sacrifices . . . even your parents. Who knows, you might grow up to become a successful inspiration to generations of athletes to come.

What if you're thinking you'll never be good enough to be an Olympian? Well, that's loser's talk! Everybody has the potential to become great at one sport, maybe even two or three. You just have to discover the sport you enjoy the most and train to become brilliant at it. You might think you're an average footballer and you're OK at swimming, but have you ever tried water polo or wrestling? Have you ever climbed to the top of a high diving board and leapt from it, or made a horse dance to music? Probably not. If you do decide to try something new, you could discover an amazing hidden talent and be ready to take on the world.

Even if you don't go on to win an Olympic gold medal, you should still be very proud of yourself for having a go and learning some incredibly useful life skills. Getting involved with sport on any level encourages you to make new friends, become part of a team, get fit and healthy, and most importantly . . . HAVE FUN! So, what are you waiting for?

ON YOUR MARKS, GET SET . . . GOLD!

TIME
13 : 00
HOME   AWAY
08 - 03

HOW DID THE OLYMPICS BEGIN?

The first thing to remember is there are two types of Summer Olympic Games — the ancient ones and the modern ones, with a 1,500-year gap between them. Since 1960, there have been Paralympic Games too. Here's a quick guide so you don't get them all muddled up.

Ancient Games

Years active: 776 BCE to 393 CE

Inventor: Ancient Greeks

Host city: Olympia

Competitors: Greek men. Women were allowed to own and train horses for equestrian events but could not compete.

Sports included: Running, boxing, wrestling, pentathlon and equestrian events.

Equipment: Not much equipment (or many clothes).

Prizes: An olive-wreath crown made of leaves from Zeus's sacred grove. No prizes for second or third place. The best of the best had statues built, and songs and stories made up about them.

Top stars:
- **Leonidas of Rhodes** – *running* – winner of 12 individual victory wreaths (a record held until 2016)
- **Cynisca of Sparta** – *equestrian, four-horse chariot* – first female victor at the Olympics, as a horse trainer
- **Milo of Croton** – *wrestling* – six-time victor, known for carrying bulls around on his shoulders and tearing trees apart

Modern Games

Years active: 1896 to present day

Inventor: Baron Pierre de Coubertin, a French aristocrat and academic. He won a gold medal in the 1912 Olympics for a poem!

Host cities: All over the world, although the Olympics has never had an African city as a host.

Competitors: Any country with a National Olympic Committee.

Sports included: See pages 10–91 to find out.

Equipment: Loads and loads, but a pair of trainers is probably the most important.

Prizes: A gold, silver or bronze medal, glory in your country, lots of appearances on TV and sponsorship deals. The best of the best still have statues built, and songs and stories made up about them.

Top stars:
- **Michael Phelps** – *USA, swimming* – 28 medals (23 gold)
- **Larisa Latynina** – *USSR, gymnastics* – 18 medals (9 gold)
- **Marit Bjørgen** – *Norway, cross-country skiing* – 15 medals (8 gold)
- **Nikolai Andrianov** – *USSR, gymnastics* – 15 medals (7 gold)

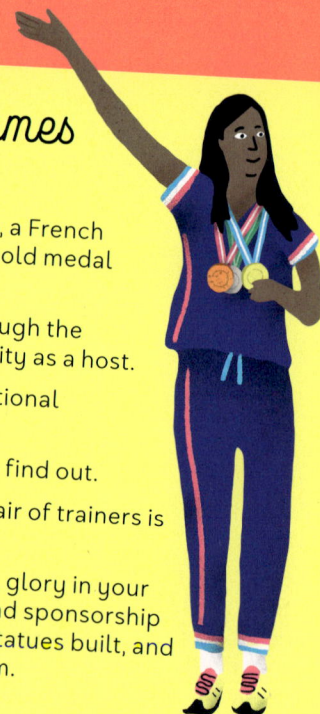

Paralympic Games

Years active: 1960 to present day

Inventor: Dr Ludwig Guttmann organised the Stoke Mandeville Games for wheelchair athletes, which later became the Paralympic Games. It wasn't called the Paralympics until 1988. 'Para' means parallel, showing that the two Games work side by side.

Host cities: In the same cities as the Olympics.

Competitors: Only wheelchair athletes competed until 1976, when it was expanded to include athletes with a much wider range of impairments.

Sports included: Almost the same as the Olympics. There are just two sports that feature only at the Paralympics — goalball and boccia.

Equipment: Depends on the sport, but some Paralympians have specially adapted equipment like running blades.

Prizes: The same as the Olympics. It's all about the medals!

Top stars:
- **Trischa Zorn** – *USA, swimming* – 55 medals (41 gold)
- **Jonas Jacobsson** – *Sweden, shooting* – 30 medals (17 gold)
- **Heinz Frei** – *Switzerland, athletics and cycling* – 35 medals (15 gold)

MODERN SUMMER OLYMPICS SO FAR

1896
ATHENS, GREECE
The first of the modern Olympics. There were 14 nations competing – now there are more than 200!

1900
PARIS, FRANCE
The first time women ever competed and there was a tug-of-war event.

1904
ST. LOUIS, USA
The first time gold, silver and bronze medals were awarded.

1908
LONDON, UK
Duelling made its first and only appearance. Competitors shot each other with wax bullets!

1912
STOCKHOLM, SWEDEN
Art events were introduced, with medals for literature, music, sculpture, painting and architecture.

1924
PARIS, FRANCE
Long-distance running was dominated by a group of athletes from Finland known as the 'Flying Finns'.

1920
ANTWERP, BELGIUM
Sweden's shooting star Oscar Swahn became the oldest Olympic medal winner ever – aged 72!

1916
BERLIN, GERMANY
Cancelled due to the First World War.

1928
AMSTERDAM, NETHERLANDS
This was the first appearance of the Olympic flame.

1932
LOS ANGELES, USA
The victory podium for medal winners appeared for the first time.

1936
BERLIN, GERMANY
The first games to have live TV coverage and the torch relay was introduced.

1940
TOKYO, JAPAN
Cancelled due to the Second World War.

1952
HELSINKI, FINLAND
Czech Emil Zátopek won gold in the 5,000 metres, the 10,000 metres and the marathon. He'd never run a marathon before!

1948
LONDON, UK
Dutch sprinter Fanny Blankers-Koen won four golds and was known as the 'Flying Housewife'.

1944
LONDON, UK
Cancelled due to the Second World War.

1956
MELBOURNE, AUSTRALIA
Due to strict rules about foreign animals being flown in, the equestrian events took place in Sweden.

1960
ROME, ITALY
The first official Paralympic Games were held this year.

1964
TOKYO, JAPAN
Ethiopia's Abebe Bikila became the first person to successfully defend the marathon title.

1968
MEXICO CITY, MEXICO
American high-jumper Dick Fosbury won gold with his new style, now known as the 'Fosbury flop'.

1980
MOSCOW, SOVIET UNION (USSR)
Sixty-six countries didn't attend for political reasons and the USSR won 195 medals.

1976
MONTREAL, CANADA
Fourteen-year-old Romanian gymnast Nadia Comãneci scored the first ever set of 'perfect 10s'.

1972
MUNICH, GERMANY
American swimmer Mark Spitz won seven gold medals – all in world-record time.

1984
LOS ANGELES, USA
USSR and 13 other countries boycotted the Games and USA won 174 medals.

1988
SEOUL, SOUTH KOREA
Swedish fencer Kerstin Palm became the first woman to take part in seven Olympic Games.

1992
BARCELONA, SPAIN
Gymnast Vitaly Scherbo from Belarus won six gold medals – including four in one day!

1996
ATLANTA, USA
American sprint and long-jump legend Carl Lewis won the last of his nine Olympic golds.

2008
BEIJING, CHINA
American swimmer Michael Phelps became the most successful athlete at a single Olympics by winning eight gold medals.

2004
ATHENS, GREECE
German kayaker Birgit Fischer won the last of her eight gold medals across six different games.

2000
SYDNEY, AUSTRALIA
British rower Sir Steve Redgrave became the first athlete to win gold medals in five Olympic Games in a row.

2012
LONDON, UK
Canadian equestrian athlete Ian Millar appeared at his tenth Olympics, a record across all Olympic sports.

2016
RIO DE JANEIRO, BRAZIL
Usain Bolt became the only sprinter to win 100-metre and 200-metre gold at three Olympics in a row.

2021
TOKYO, JAPAN
Originally planned for 2020, this was delayed a year by the COVID-19 pandemic. No fans were allowed in stadiums.

2024
PARIS, FRANCE
Breaking and kitesurfing make their first appearance. Tahiti, a far-off French territory in the Pacific Ocean, hosts all surfing events.

BASKETBALL

WHAT IS IT?

A team sport where really, really tall people hurl a big orange ball through a hoop hung high in the air.

The Rules

Two teams of five have to shoot the ball through their opponent's basketball hoop. To move the ball forward, players dribble by bouncing the ball on the floor, or by passing it to one of their teammates. It's two points for shots inside the three-point line, and three points for those outside. Pushing and shoving the other team isn't allowed, although it's very easy to do. The team with the most points at the end of four quarters wins.

THE HISTORY BIT

Basketball wasn't invented until 1891, using a peach basket as a net, so it's a relatively young sport. It quickly spread through universities across the USA and then across the world, and was so popular it became an Olympic sport in 1936. Wheelchair basketball has been at the Paralympics since the first Games in 1960. 3x3 basketball arrived in 2020.

HEADBAND
Basketball is a sweaty sport; these stop you dripping all over the court.

GOGGLES
If your eyesight isn't good then these are a must.

A CLOSER LOOK

SCORING HOOP
This is 46 centimetres wide and strong enough for players to hang from during dunks.

BIG TRAINERS
Support your ankles and the air-cushioned soles help with higher leaps.

FREE-THROW LINE
Players shoot from here after being fouled. Shots are worth one point each.

BASIC TRAINING

Bouncing a ball is a natural thing to do, so now do it lots of times while running. After you've run around a bit, stop and throw the ball at the top of a very high wall. When you're comfortable doing this, add loads of tricks so you look cool.

UPSIDES

It's fast and high scoring. Games never end 0–0. They're more likely to end 98–102 and that's a lot of baskets. Even if you're not very good, there's a chance you might score. Just chuck the ball up there and see what happens.

DOWNSIDES

Some basketball players will hog the ball, so it can feel like you're spending all your time running up and down the court without ever getting a touch.

BACKBOARD
Always clear, so people sitting behind still get a good view of the action.

BALL
In the past, balls were heavy and bounced all over the place. Now they're much lighter, but still bounce all over the place.

BASKET
This has a hole cut out of the bottom, so isn't really much of a basket.

SKILLS NEEDED
Anyone can play basketball, but it helps if you're tall. The average height for male players is 6 foot 7 inches, or 202 centimetres. The average height for female players is 6 feet, or 185 centimetres. So height is a plus, but so are speed, agility and ball-handling skills.

Height is not important in wheelchair basketball, but you do need good balance and strong wrists, shoulders and arms.

INJURIES
With all that twisting, pivoting and jumping, basketball players get a lot of ankle and foot injuries. That large ball also hurts like mad if it hits you on the tops of your fingers, so make sure you learn how to catch it properly.

Sound Like a Pro
"ALLEY-OOP"
– A player catching a pass in mid-air and slamming it down into the basket.

"DUNK"
– Slamming the ball through the hoop.

"TRAVELLING"
– Running with the ball in your hands, instead of bouncing it. Foul!

"BUZZER-BEATER"
– A shot made in the final second of a game.

THE PAINT
If you are attacking, don't hang around in here for more than three seconds or the ball is given to the opposition.

THREE-POINT LINE
Shoot from behind here to score three points, everything inside the three-point arc is worth two points.

CHANCE OF BECOMING A CHAMPION
Slim   OK   Good   Great

Very hard. Basketball is one of the most popular sports in the world, with over 20 million people playing in the USA alone. You'd better start training now.

BEST EVER
Unsurprisingly, USA has dominated Olympic basketball in both men and women's events. They've won 30 medals, 25 of them gold. Russia are next up with just 12.

FOOTBALL

WHAT IS IT?

Two teams of 11 try and kick a ball past a goalkeeper and into the opposition's net to score a goal. After scoring, they celebrate wildly or do a silly dance.

The Rules

Football has loads of rules nowadays, but basically two teams must kick or head the ball into the other team's net. Only the goalkeepers are allowed to touch the ball with their hands, and only in their own area. You can't foul your opponents or you will get sent off the pitch.

SKILLS NEEDED

All kinds of skills can be applied to being a top footballer, but not all of them are vital. It helps if goalkeepers are tall and good with their hands. Defenders should be tough and good at tackling and heading. Midfielders should be quick, able to do tricks, and good at passing and tackling. Strikers should be fast and good at shooting.

THE HISTORY BIT

A version of football began in China in 300 BCE and since then various ancient civilisations have played ball games using their feet. However, it wasn't until the Middle Ages in the UK that football took off, and proper rules were drawn up by the Football Association in 1863. Football first appeared in the Olympics in 1900, but only three teams entered and nobody won a medal. Five-a-side football has been at the Paralympics since 2004.

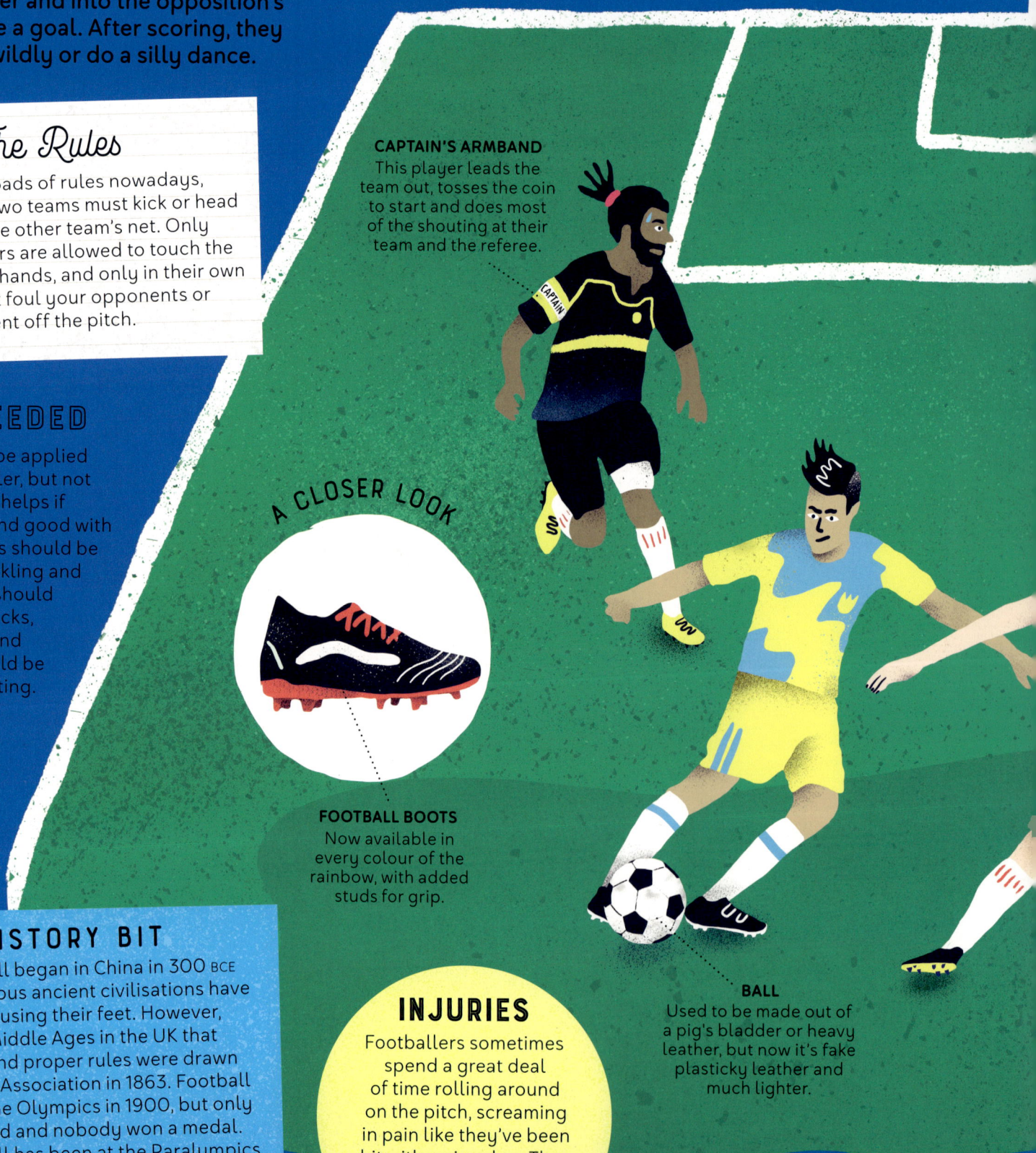

GOALPOSTS
7.32 metres across and 2.44 metres high, so perfect for swinging on if you are a bored keeper when all the action is at the other end of the pitch.

CAPTAIN'S ARMBAND
This player leads the team out, tosses the coin to start and does most of the shouting at their team and the referee.

A CLOSER LOOK

FOOTBALL BOOTS
Now available in every colour of the rainbow, with added studs for grip.

INJURIES

Footballers sometimes spend a great deal of time rolling around on the pitch, screaming in pain like they've been hit with an iron bar. Then moments later they are totally fine. This is known as diving.

BALL
Used to be made out of a pig's bladder or heavy leather, but now it's fake plasticky leather and much lighter.

NET
Stops the ball flying into the crowd and hitting them in the face.

Slim	OK	Good	Great

Football is the most popular sport in the world. Everyone wants to be a professional footballer.

GOALKEEPING GLOVES
Protect fingers and help keepers get a better grip on the ball.

RED CARD
Get one of these and you are sent off and have to go back to the changing rooms for a little cry.

REFEREE
The person in charge of the match.

UPSIDES
Footballers are among some of the richest and most famous people in the world.

DOWNSIDES
Being rich and famous sometimes isn't all that it's cracked up to be.

BASIC TRAINING
Get a ball — it doesn't matter how big or small — and practise juggling it, using your feet and head. Try to keep it off the floor. Then find a wall and shoot the ball at the wall as many times as you can. In your head, pretend you're scoring the winning goal in the final.

Sound Like a Pro

"NUTMEG"
— Passing the ball through your opponent's legs and collecting it on the other side.

"RABONA"
— Kicking the ball by wrapping your foot around the back side of your standing leg.

"TIKI-TAKA"
— A style of play with short, quick passing and movement.

"ROW Z"
— Booting the ball as far away into the crowd as possible to waste time.

"UNDERDOG"
— A team that isn't expected to win, not one that spends the game hiding under a dog.

SHIN PADS
Protective covering for shins worn under socks, so great when tackled.

BEST EVER
The queens of Olympic football are the USA team, who have won four gold medals and one silver. In the men's tournament, Hungary have won three golds, a silver and a bronze, while Brazil have the most medals with seven, but only two of them are gold.

Goalball

WHAT IS IT?

A team sport where players roll a hard rubber ball, with two bells in it, towards a large goal in an attempt to score.

The History Bit

Goalball was invented after the Second World War to help visually impaired soldiers with their recovery. It was so popular that it became a men's Paralympic sport in 1976, and women's in 1984. Goalball is one of only two Paralympic sports that doesn't have a matching sport at the Olympics.

SKILLS NEEDED

To generate power when they roll the ball, many goalball players use a 360-degree turn-and-roll technique. This sometimes causes the ball to bounce slightly, making it harder to stop.

Players need a lot of skill, tactical knowledge and split-second reactions. There's hardly a moment to take a breather.

The Rules

The aim of goalball is to score as many goals as possible, in two 12-minute halves, by rolling the ball into your opponent's net. The defending team tries to block the ball with their bodies, usually at full stretch. It's like having three goalies.

It's a very fast-flowing game. Each team has three players on the court at a time, with three substitutes, and teams have just ten seconds to throw the ball back to the other team. Balls can reach speeds of 80 kilometres per hour! The crowd needs to be totally silent when the ball is in play, so the players can hear the ball and each other, but cheering is allowed when a goal is scored.

A CLOSER LOOK

EYESHADES

Goalball is played by athletes who may have varying degrees of visual impairments, so every player wears blackout eyeshades to keep things even. Athletes can't touch their eyeshades without permission from the referee.

INJURIES

Goalball players will use any part of their body to stop the ball going in the net, so be prepared to get bashed in the face by the ball.

UPSIDES

There are very few sports exclusively for visually impaired athletes. It moves quickly, and with only three players on each side, you are always in the thick of the action.

DOWNSIDES

You will spend most of the game on the floor. Also, the bigger the crowd, the harder it is to keep them quiet.

LARGE, LONG GOAL
The goal stretches the whole width of the 9-metre playing area.

HIP PADDING, KNEE AND ELBOW PADS AND CHEST PROTECTORS
Because athletes spend a lot of time on the court floor.

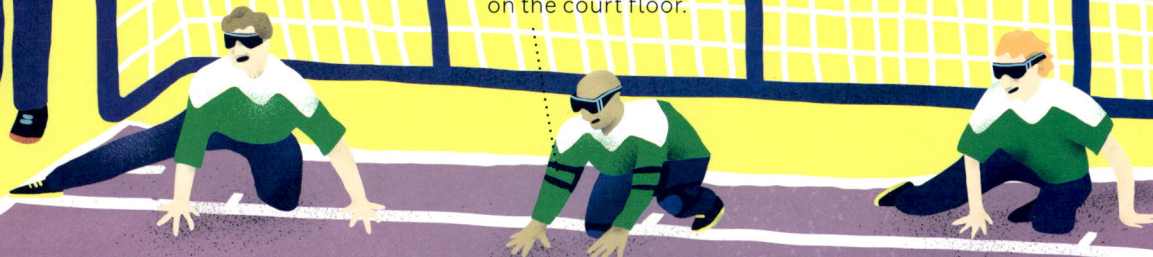

LARGE RUBBER BALL WITH TWO BELLS IN IT
The sound helps the players follow the ball.

STRING
The court is marked out with string to help players know where they are.

OFFICIALS
There are more officials than players on the court: two referees, plus goal judges, timers and scorers.

Sound Like a Pro

"DISCUS THROW"
— When a player crouches down, rotates 360 degrees and releases the ball so it bounces near to them. Designed to bamboozle the defenders.

"HIGH-ARM DISCUS THROW"
— When a player stays upright and does a discus throw. Even more bamboozling.

"BRAZILIAN SPECIAL"
— When a player throws the ball backwards between their legs towards the opposing goal.

BEST EVER

Goalball used to be a very open competition, with no one country dominating the leaderboard. However, USA currently tops the medal table with a whopping 13 medals across the men's and women's events — however, they only have three gold medals. Finland and Denmark can hold their heads high with three golds also.

BASIC TRAINING

Tie a scarf over your eyes, get a family member to ring a bell in your house and see if you can find it in a couple of seconds. Avoid having the bell thrown at you as this might hurt.

CHANCE OF BECOMING A CHAMPION

| Slim | OK | Good | Great |

If you have a visual impairment, goalball is a great sport to get involved with. Start young and your chances of making it to the Paralympics are greatly increased.

RUGBY

WHAT IS IT?

A team sport where players move an oval-shaped ball over the goal line by passing it backwards to each other.

A CLOSER LOOK

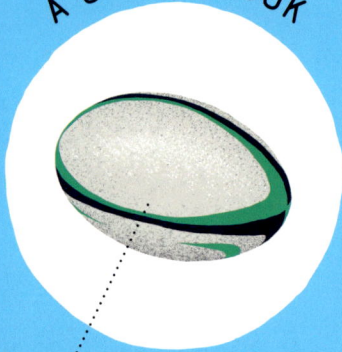

RUGBY BALL
Covered in dimples for good grip, so players can pass with speed and accuracy.

SKILLS NEEDED

Rugby players need to be strong, quick, good at ball handling and tackling, and have loads of stamina.

SCRUM CAP
Help to prevent ear damage – cauliflower ear is a common injury for rugby players.

MOUTHGUARD
To prevent your teeth getting knocked out.

CLOSE-FITTING, LIGHTWEIGHT VESTS
Harder to grab than the cotton jerseys players used to wear.

MUD
If you don't like getting muddy, then rugby is not the sport for you.

STURDY, STUDDED BOOTS
For grip when running or crashing into players on muddy ground.

Sound Like a Pro

"GARRYOWEN" or **"BOMB"**
– A high, short kick into the air.

"BLOOD BIN"
– A substitute player who comes on to the pitch to temporarily replace a player who is bleeding.

"HAKA"
– A traditional Māori dance, usually done by New Zealand teams before a game to try and intimidate their opponents.

"HOSPITAL PASS"
– A terrible pass that usually results in the receiver getting tackled.

CHANCE OF BECOMING A CHAMPION

Slim — OK — Good — Great

Rugby is growing across the world, but it's still only played at a very high standard by a handful of countries like New Zealand, Australia, South Africa and the UK.

The History Bit

The ancient Roman game *harpastum*, and medieval versions of 'football' involved carrying the ball. However, it's the story of a schoolboy from Rugby, who invented the game in 1823 by picking up a football and running with it, that's famous all over the world.

Rugby joined the Olympics as a 15-player sport in 1900, but then only appeared occasionally after that. The seven-player version of the game made its Olympic debut in 2016. Wheelchair rugby, or 'murderball', became a Paralympic sport in 2000.

BASIC TRAINING

Sit on a football until it's gone into a wonky shape, pick it up and start bashing into things. Try the sofa cushions first, as most other stuff tends to hurt.

SHORT SHORTS
To match the vest.

The Rules

Olympic rugby is the 'sevens' version of the game, rather than the traditional 15-player game. Two teams of seven play two seven-minute halves on a full-sized rugby pitch. Players can score a try for five points by placing the ball behind one of the goal lines at either end of the pitch. They can get an extra two points by kicking the ball over the H-shaped posts for a conversion. There are three points available for a drop goal, and three for a converted penalty – both must go over the posts. Players can carry the ball in their hands, but only pass to another player by throwing it backwards.

Wheelchair rugby uses a round ball, is played indoors and only four players from each mixed team are allowed on the court at one time. Matches are four eight-minute quarters. Players who have the ball must pass or bounce the ball within ten seconds. Athletes try to tackle the ball from each other's laps or by smashing the wheelchairs into each other. This can create havoc, with wheelchairs tipping up all over the court.

INJURIES

Rugby is a full-contact sport so injuries are many and varied. Forwards get injured the most as they're involved in lots of tackles. Strains, bruises, fractures and broken bones are common.

UPSIDES

Charging your way downfield with the ball, riding tackles and bashing into people to score a try is great fun.

DOWNSIDES

If you're not quick enough, you can get bashed about a lot.

Wheelchair Rugby

GLOVES WITH ADDED STICKY GRIP
In wheelchair rugby, gloves are an important part of the kit.

BOUNCY BALL
This is a bit like a volleyball with a special surface to add grip.

BEST EVER

Fiji are the masters of rugby sevens and and have won both gold medals so far in the men's tournament. New Zealand and Australia have a gold each in the women's event. USA have the most wheelchair rugby medals with seven in total, three of them gold.

COMPETITION WHEELCHAIR
There are two types — one for attacking players and one for defenders.

HANDBALL

WHAT IS IT?

A super-fast ball sport, where teams of seven try and score as many goals as possible by throwing the ball into a large net with one hand.

The Rules

Players are only allowed to take three steps or have the ball for three seconds before they have to pass, shoot or dribble it. Shots on goal must be from outside the goal area, however attacking players can go in the area if they are flying through the air and not touching the floor. This is known as a dive or jump shot. The poor goalkeeper usually doesn't stand a chance against these and that's why teams score between 25 and 40 goals a game.

GOAL
About 2 metres high, with its posts and crossbar painted in red and white stripes.

JUMP SHOT
Powerful flying shot. Take that, keeper!

LIGHT SHOES
Players can wear any kind of trainer, as long as they don't leave marks on the court.

A CLOSER LOOK

SMALL, SOFT BALL
Easy to grip and catch with only one hand.

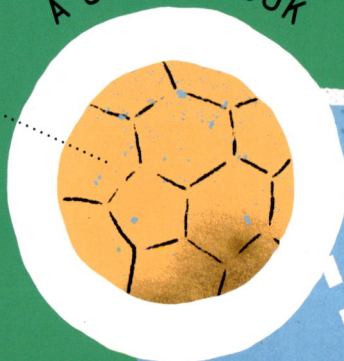

BASIC TRAINING

If you want to be an outfield player, jump high off the third step from the bottom on your staircase at home while throwing a honeydew melon with one hand towards the ground. Make sure you clean up afterwards.

If you want to be a goalkeeper, get your family to throw balls at you as fast as possible from point-blank range. Wildly fling your arms and legs around, and if you are lucky, one of them might hit you.

SKILLS NEEDED

Height is a big advantage in handball, especially if you're a goalkeeper. You also need to be fast and agile. Handball players spend a lot of time jumping in the air to hurl the ball at the goal, so an explosive shot helps too. To be a goalkeeper, you must be good at star jumps, spreading yourself as wide as possible, hoping that one day you might be able to save something.

The History Bit

Handball was first played in Germany and Scandinavia in the late 19th century, although it took until 1917 for someone to properly write down the rules. It first appeared at the Olympics in 1936 then didn't reappear until 1972. The women's competition was close behind, making its debut in 1976.

NO GLOVES
It's easier to throw the ball without gloves, but players sometimes wear strapping around their thumbs and fingers to prevent injury.

STAR JUMP
Goalkeepers do this a lot to try and stop the other team scoring.

"CENTRE BACK" — A creative player who directs play in defence and attack. Usually the best player in the team.

"ASSAULT" — A body foul on another player.

"SAVE" — Goalies sometimes do one of these! Make sure you cheer when it happens.

"PISTON MOVEMENT" — Attacking play that moves forwards and backwards.

BEST EVER

There's a good spread of medals across Europe, but France are on top of the men's tournament with five — three of them gold. In the women's tournament, Denmark have three golds, but Norway and South Korea are close behind with two golds each, and six medals each in total.

GOALIE PANTS
Goalkeepers wear these because it can get a bit chilly in those sports halls.

INJURIES
Ankle and knee injuries are common — there's even an injury called jumper's knee. You'll notice lots of players wearing knee pads and strappings.

UPSIDES
Handball is fast and fun, and there are plenty of chances to score lots of goals.

DOWNSIDES
Being a goalkeeper.

CHANCE OF BECOMING A CHAMPION

Slim	OK	Good	Great

Handball is one of the most popular games that people play in Europe, so the chances of becoming a pro there are slim. However, in some countries it's not a very common sport.

HOCKEY

WHAT IS IT?

Sometimes called field hockey, in this game two teams of 11 try and hit a ball into their opponents' goal using a wooden stick.

The Rules

Using the flat side of your stick, dribble, pass, flick and sweep the ball along the ground towards the semicircle around your opponents' goal. Then have a shot and see if you can beat the goalkeeper. The team with the most goals at the end of the match is the winner. Only the goalkeeper can touch the ball with their body and you can't swing your stick around like you're going into battle.

INJURIES

Hand and forearm injuries are common because they're closest to the sticks. All the leaning down can also put pressure on your back.

THE HISTORY BIT

There are carvings of ancient Greeks playing what looks like hockey from 510 BCE, but historians have disagreed about where the game came from for centuries. What we do know is that the modern version of hockey was developed in Great Britain in the 19th century and made it to the Olympics in 1908 for men, and 1980 for women.

Basic Training

Find a walking stick and a hard apple, like a Granny Smith. Then, using the stick, dribble the apple all the way home without kicking it or picking it up. Once you get there, whack it as hard as you can through the open front door. If you break something, blame the International Hockey Federation.

BANDANA

Very popular in hockey. Players spend most of the time looking down, so the bandana keeps their hair out of their eyes. After the match they can tie it over their face to rob a bank.

A CLOSER LOOK

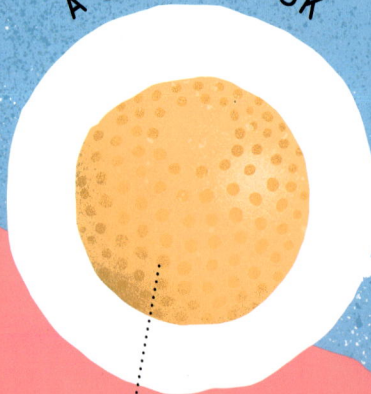

HARD PLASTIC BALL

Can be whacked at ferocious speeds of around 100 kilometres per hour. It also has tiny bumps to stop it skidding on a wet field.

BEST EVER

In the men's game, hockey is easily India's best sport, with 12 medals, eight of them gold. In the women's tournament, the Netherlands have nine medals, four gold.

PITCH
Usually green or blue artificial turf, with a covering of water or sand to make the game quicker.

Sound Like a Pro

"BULLY-OFF"
– Two players must touch sticks before they can get the ball. This is done to start or restart the game.

"RUSHER"
– The player chosen to charge at the attacker taking a penalty corner.

"HACKING"
– Whacking another player's stick rather than the ball.

"GREEN CARD"
– A warning card, before the yellow and red cards.

GLOVES
These help with gripping the stick and protecting the hands from injury.

GOAL
Rectangle-shaped goal, with a backboard and sideboards.

LONG SHIN PADS
Getting hit on the shins with a wooden stick really hurts. Wear these and it won't hurt quite as much.

STICK
A J-shaped, hook-bottomed stick, perfect for close ball control.

GOALKEEPER
Dressed in so much protective clothing it's hard to walk — helmet, chest, neck and arm guards, padded shorts, huge leg guards and big kicker boots.

UPSIDES
Hockey is fast, energetic and a great team sport.

DOWNSIDES
Keeping up with the ball can be incredibly tiring and the ball really hurts if it whacks into you.

SKILLS NEEDED
You need stamina to keep running up and down the pitch and good hand–eye coordination. You must be able to make quick decisions and bravery helps too — especially if you're defending a penalty corner.

CHANCE OF BECOMING A CHAMPION

Slim	OK	Good	Great

Hockey is a very popular sport across the globe, played by over 100 countries in five different continents. However, with 11 players on a team there are a lot of opportunities to grab one of the positions.

Boccia

WHAT IS IT?

A ball sport for athletes with physical disabilities, where you need to get your ball close to a target ball. Everyone thinks it's a bit like bowls, but it's better than that.

The Rules

Matches are divided into a number of ends or frames. In each end, an athlete throws their set of balls as close as possible to the jack, or target ball. The player whose ball is closest to the jack after all the balls are thrown scores a point, and extra points for any other ball that they have nearer than their opponent's closest ball.

Balls can be thrown, chucked, rolled or even kicked in any way you fancy. You can even hurl it down like a cricket fast-bowler if you wish.

Individual players and pairs play four ends, and teams of three play six ends. After all ends have been played, the athletes with the highest score win the match.

A CLOSER LOOK

BALLS
A set of six red or blue soft leather balls, which can roll but don't bounce, as well as a white target ball called a jack.

NUMBERS
Athletes are identified by numbers attached to their wheelchairs or legs.

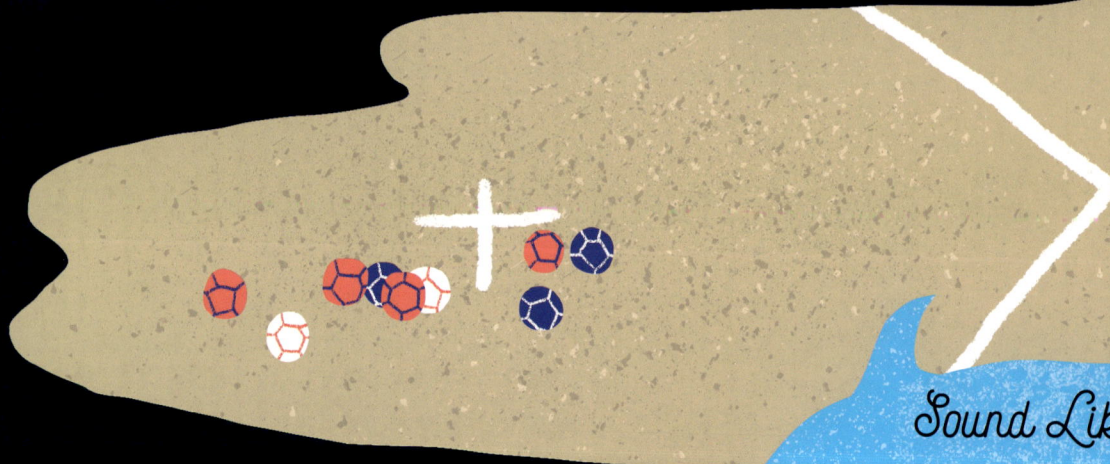

Sound Like a Pro

"SPOCKING" or "BOMBING"
– A hard underarm bowling type aimed at directly hitting the balls or the jack.

"KISS"
– When a ball is touching the jack.

"SKUNKED"
– When a team scores no points.

"PALLINO"
– Another term for the jack.

"CASINO"
– Scoring all four points in one frame.

"JACK ADVANTAGE"
– The player who gets to throw the jack and the first ball has this.

"LAGGING" or "POINTING"
– An underarm action rolling the ball towards the jack.

THE HISTORY BIT

Boccia has its origins in ancient Greece and Egypt, where players threw large stones at a stone target. The Italians turned it into something called *bocce*, which means 'bowls', and it spread across the world a bit like similar games from England and France — bowls and *pétanque*. Boccia joined the Paralympics in 1984 and is one of two Paralympic sports that doesn't have a similar sport in the Olympics.

Skills Needed

Boccia is for players with cerebral palsy and impairments that affect motor skills. You need to be strong to spend hours leaning over the side of the wheelchair, and your shoulders will get sore. Mental toughness is also very important because you're put under nail-biting pressure to land a ball just millimetres away from the jack. Boccia is also a great test of muscle control, strategy and pin-point accuracy.

UPSIDES

It's a top-notch strategy sport that is hard to master. It looks easy, but it isn't. It's also a mixed sport so men and women can play together.

DOWNSIDES

Boccia requires lots and lots of practice, and stacks of concentration.

HEAD POINTER
Helps athletes who can't use their hands push the ball down the ramp.

INJURIES

You'll be very unlucky if you get injured playing Boccia. The referee measuring the ball distances is more likely to get injured by a stray throw.

WHEELCHAIR
It doesn't require a special chair to play, so it's not an expensive sport to get involved with.

RAMP
Some athletes are allowed to use ramps to help roll the ball, or the help of an assistant if they can't move the ball on their own.

BEST EVER

Portugal top the medal table with 27 medals, eight of them gold. However, South Korea have the most gold medals, with ten out of their total 23-medal haul.

CHANCE OF BECOMING A CHAMPION

| Slim | OK | Good | Great |

Tough but not impossible. Boccia is highly skilled at the top level, however it's a very popular sport and there are lots of opportunities to get involved. It's played in around 50 countries.

BASIC TRAINING

Boccia is the perfect game to practise in the garden, but you'll need to make sure you raid the fruit bowl first. Sitting in a chair, throw an orange across your back garden. Then, aiming as best you can, try and land six lemons as close as possible to the orange. Oranges and lemons love Boccia — it's either that or going rotten back in the kitchen.

VOLLEYBALL

WHAT IS IT?

Two teams battle it out, either side of a high net, trying to stop a ball hitting the floor.

BASIC TRAINING

Cover your lounge floor in sand, throw a beach ball in the air and try to stop it from hitting the ground by whacking it with your hands clenched together. When your parents get home and find out what you've done to the carpet, hide behind the sofa.

LIBERO
Specialist defensive player wearing a different colour to everyone else in the team.

VOLLEYBALL
A soft-ish bouncy ball.

A CLOSER LOOK

VERY HIGH NET
The net is 2.4 metres tall for men and 2.2 metres tall for women.

KNEE PADS
To prevent grazes when players dive for the ball.

OPPOSITE HITTER
The player in this position tries to gain points against the other team while also playing defence.

VESTS AND SHORT SHORTS
Usually lightweight cotton with a number on the back.

The Rules

Indoor volleyball has two teams of six, who get up to three touches or 'volleys' to keep the ball off the floor on their side of the net, and then land it on the floor on their opponent's side of the court. The first team to 25 points wins the set, and it's usually best of five sets.

Beach volleyball has similar rules, but there are only two players on each team. It's played on a slightly smaller, sandy court, with a softer, smaller ball and it's best of three games.

Sitting volleyball is similar to indoor volleyball, but has a smaller court and lower net, and players must have a part of their pelvis touching the floor when playing a shot.

INJURIES

Shoulder and finger injuries are common, along with sunburn if you forget to put suncream on for beach volleyball.

THE HISTORY BIT

Volleyball was invented in 1895 in the USA as a less tough version of basketball. Its popularity quickly spread around the world. It wasn't made an Olympic sport until 1964. Beach volleyball was invented in 1915 and became an Olympic sport in 1996. The Paralympics added sitting volleyball in 1980 for men and 2004 for women.

Sitting Volleyball

PELVIS ON THE GROUND
At all times, otherwise you'll get a 'lifting' foul.

REFEREE ON A PLATFORM
There are usually two referees. The senior referee stands up on a platform to get a better view.

SETTER
Player in charge of making team decisions and coming up with a plan of attack.

Sound Like a Pro

"SPIKE"
– To smash the ball into your opponents' court.

"KONG"
– A one-handed block.

"SPATCH"
– When you hit the ball and it ends up somewhere unexpected.

"SPALDING"
– When a player gets hit really hard in the face or body by the ball.

"CAMPFIRE"
– When a serve lands in between two beach volleyball players because they couldn't decide who should go for it.

SKILLS NEEDED

Being tall is an advantage, but you also need to have lightning-quick reflexes to get into the right position to block, dig, set and spike.

BEST EVER

In indoor volleyball, the Soviet Union (USSR) tops the leaderboard with 12 medals. However, as the Soviet Union no longer exists, Brazil and USA, who both have 11 medals, can overtake. Those two countries also domiate beach volleyball! USA's Misty May-Treanor and teammate Kerri Walsh Jennings are the queens of the sand with three golds. In sitting volleyball, Iran has seven gold medals.

MAY-TREANOR AND WALSH JENNINGS' MEDAL COUNT: 🥇 X 3

UPSIDES
Nothing beats leaping like a salmon above the net to smash down a powerful spike into your opponents' court. KABOOM . . . take that!

DOWNSIDES
Diving around to return the ball can give you floor burns or a mouthful of sand depending on which type of volleyball you play.

CHANCE OF BECOMING A CHAMPION

Slim	OK	Good	↑ Great

Many people enjoy messing about with a volleyball on a beach, but it's not as popular when it comes to forming a team and taking it seriously. It has done well in eastern Europe and Brazil, but other 'tall people' sports like basketball and handball are pinching a lot of the players.

GOLF

WHAT IS IT?

Spending most of the day outside trying to hit a tiny white ball into 18 little holes with a range of different metal clubs.

BASIC TRAINING

Get a small ball about the size of an apricot. Actually, why not just get an apricot. Then find a stick that has a sticky out bit at the bottom. Hit the apricot as hard as you can across a field and into some deep undergrowth. Spend 30 minutes looking for the apricot, then give up and go inside.

SINGLE GLOVE
Often worn for better grip.

CADDIE
Carries the golf bag around for a player, offers advice and support. Tells them what they should have for lunch.

COLOURFUL CLOTHING
Colour-wise, anything goes. If you want to wear a purple waistcoat, lime green trousers and yellow socks at the same time, then this is the sport for you.

INJURIES
Shoulder, elbow and back pain is very common, although probably more so for the caddie who has to carry your bag.

CLUBS
Come in a range of sizes and shapes, called woods, irons, wedges and putters.

Sound Like a Pro

"WHIFF"
– Attempting to hit the ball, but totally missing it.

"PAR"
– The standard number of strokes it should take to finish a hole. Usually three, four or five.

"BOGEY"
– One stroke over par. So not a good thing.

"DOGLEG"
– Where the shape of the hole looks like a dog's leg – straight with a bend at the end.

"PLUS FOURS"
– A pair of baggy knickerbocker-style trousers that end just under the knee.

BEST EVER

Golf hasn't been a part of many Olympics over the years so only a handful of medals have been handed out. USA have four golds, two for men and two for women – although two of those medals were awarded in 1900.

A CLOSER LOOK

FLAG
A very serious flag. Don't wave it around or other golfers will tut at you.

GREEN
Where the hole lives. A very precious bit of grass, a bit like a posh carpet, so don't go running and dancing on it.

HOLE
So small it has to have a big flag poking out of it so you can spot what you are aiming at from far away.

BALL
A small, hard ball covered in over 300 dimples that help the ball travel further. Usually white, but luminous colours are popular as it makes them easier to find.

BUNKER
Try and keep your ball out of these sandpits. Sadly, not a place for sandcastles.

FAIRWAY
The part of the course between the tee and the green, surrounded by rough which it's easy to lose your ball (and your temper) in.

SKILLS NEEDED

Golfers come in all shapes and sizes. Because the caddie carries your bag and some golfers drive around in little buggies, you don't have to be super fit like other Olympic athletes.

To play golf, you need to be mentally tough because you're basically in a battle with yourself across 18 holes. If you're the kind of person who loses your temper when you burn your toast, then golf isn't for you.

TEE
Drive your ball off the top of this little plastic or wooden stick at the start of every hole.

The History Bit

It is believed golf started in Scotland in the 15th century, where players whacked a pebble around a course using a stick. However, some historians trace it back to an ancient Roman game called *paganica*. Golf first appeared at the Olympics in 1900. It made it to 1904, before disappearing off the event list for over 100 years and making a comeback in 2016.

UPSIDES

Golfers get to wear casual clothes, travel to play on some of the most beautiful courses in the world and don't need to do any running.

DOWNSIDES

Golfers play in all weathers. Trying to find your ball in the woods while it's cold and rainy is not fun. And there are more rules than most sports.

CHANCE OF BECOMING A CHAMPION

Slim   OK   Good   Great

World-class professional golfers enter the Olympics, so in order to qualify, you probably need to start winning tournaments now.

Shooting

SKEET
In skeet shooting, clay discs are fired from a machine called a trap. Shooters need lightning-quick reactions to hit them.

WHAT IS IT?

Very serious athletes stand very still and fire rifles, shotguns and pistols at teeny-tiny targets and hope they don't miss.

A CLOSER LOOK

SPECIAL SHOOTING GLASSES
A complicated set of glasses with different lenses to help the eyes focus, and blinders to block any distractions.

The Rules

Rifle and pistol-shooting events are held on a shooting range, where competitors fire at targets 10, 25 and 50 metres away. Points are awarded depending on how close to the bullseye you get.

Skeet shooters fire shotguns at moving clay targets called pigeons or skeets, that are pinged across the sky at different angles and directions. You've just got to keep hitting them — the more you miss, the trickier it is to get a medal.

CLOTHING THAT MAKES YOU LOOK LIKE YOU'RE FROM THE FUTURE
Everything is designed to stop even the slightest movement, like a puff of wind, distracting you.

SHOTGUN
Shotguns have different length barrels depending on the event. Magnifying lenses are not allowed.

AIR RIFLE
Looks like a gun from outer space.

INJURIES
Pain in the neck, back, hips and knees is common because you have to stand and kneel for long periods of time and support a heavy rifle.

BASIC TRAINING
Find a room with a dirty mark on the wall, then stand on the other side of the room and stare at it for two hours without moving.

KNEE ROLLS
Shooters wear stiff canvas trousers and jackets. The trousers have non-slip rubber patches on the knees to keep the shooters steady when they're kneeling or lying down.

SKILLS NEEDED

Shooting is all about being cool, calm and collected. If you're easily distracted by things like clouds, birds, wind or someone coughing a kilometre away, then shooting probably isn't for you. You need to remain as still as a lamp post, be able to control your breathing and not scratch your itchy chin. Good eyesight, great aim, stamina, strength and nerves of steel are also crucial.

UPSIDES
Hitting the bullseye in any sport is a great feeling. In shooting, you will hit loads of bullseyes, plus you get to dress like a cyborg.

DOWNSIDES
Shooting involves extreme pressure, and standing still and remaining calm can be very hard — especially if your opponents are trying to distract you by saying, "Look at that cloud, it looks like a baboon!"

DISTANCE
Rifle and pistol targets are 10, 25 or 50 metres away from the competitors, depending on the event.

RIFLE TARGET
Digital sensors in the target send information to the scorers. The bullseye is the size of your little fingernail.

PISTOL TARGET
You'll lose points if you accidentally hit someone else's target!

AIR PISTOL
The arm that holds the pistol must be straight and completely unsupported.

Sound Like a Pro

"FIRING LINE" – Where you stand to shoot.

"TRAP" – The machine that fires the clay targets into the air.

"PULL" or "HUP" or "READY" – Skeet shooters shout this so the clay target may be released into the air.

"MUZZLE" – The front end of the weapon where the pellet/bullet/round leaves it.

BEST EVER

USA dominates the shooting medal table with a whopping 116 medals, 57 of them gold. American marksman Carl Osburn had 11 shooting medals (five gold) from the 1912, 1920 and 1924 Olympics. At the Paralympics, Swedish shooter Jonas Jacobsson has a huge tally of 30 medals, 17 gold.

OSBURN'S MEDAL COUNT:
1 X5   2 X4   3 X2

The History Bit

The Chinese probably introduced guns to the world in the 10th century, when they invented gunpowder. Then various weapons started appearing across the world and soon armies swapped their bows and arrows for rifles and pistols.

Shooting became a sport around 500 years ago, when people realised it wasn't just for killing things and could be fun. It was one of the sports at the 1896 Olympics and joined the Paralympics in 1976.

CHANCE OF BECOMING A CHAMPION

Slim | OK | Good | Great

Shooting obviously has a lot of restrictions. You can't just pick up a gun and start shooting at things — that will get you sent to prison. However, if you're taught properly, your chances increase greatly as it's not a sport that many people learn.

ARCHERY

WHAT IS IT?

Using a bow, you shoot arrows at a far-away target. It's basically playing Robin Hood without the hiding in trees bit.

Sound Like a Pro

"UPSHOT" – The last shot in an archery tournament.

"LOOSE" – The act of shooting the arrow.

"LITTLE JOHN" – Best friend of Robin Hood . . . Hang on, how did this get in here?

"QUIVER" – Where you put all your arrows.

"NOCK" – Putting the arrow in the bow.

"FLETCHER" – Someone who makes arrows. So, anyone you know called Fletcher had ancestors who did this job.

A CLOSER LOOK

ARROW FLIGHTS
Once made of feathers, arrow flights are now made of plastic and help with speed and direction.

BOW
A bit like a longbow from the olden days, but now made of carbon fibre.

BOWSTRING
The archer pulls this back with three fingers to touch their face.

BUCKET HAT
Soft, practical protection from the sun.

SUNGLASSES
So the sun doesn't get in the archer's eyes.

TABS
Protect the archer's fingers.

ARM GUARD
A brace which protects the inside of an archer's arm from the dreaded string slap.

QUIVER OF ARROWS
Kept on the same side as the archer's drawing hand, so they can reload easily.

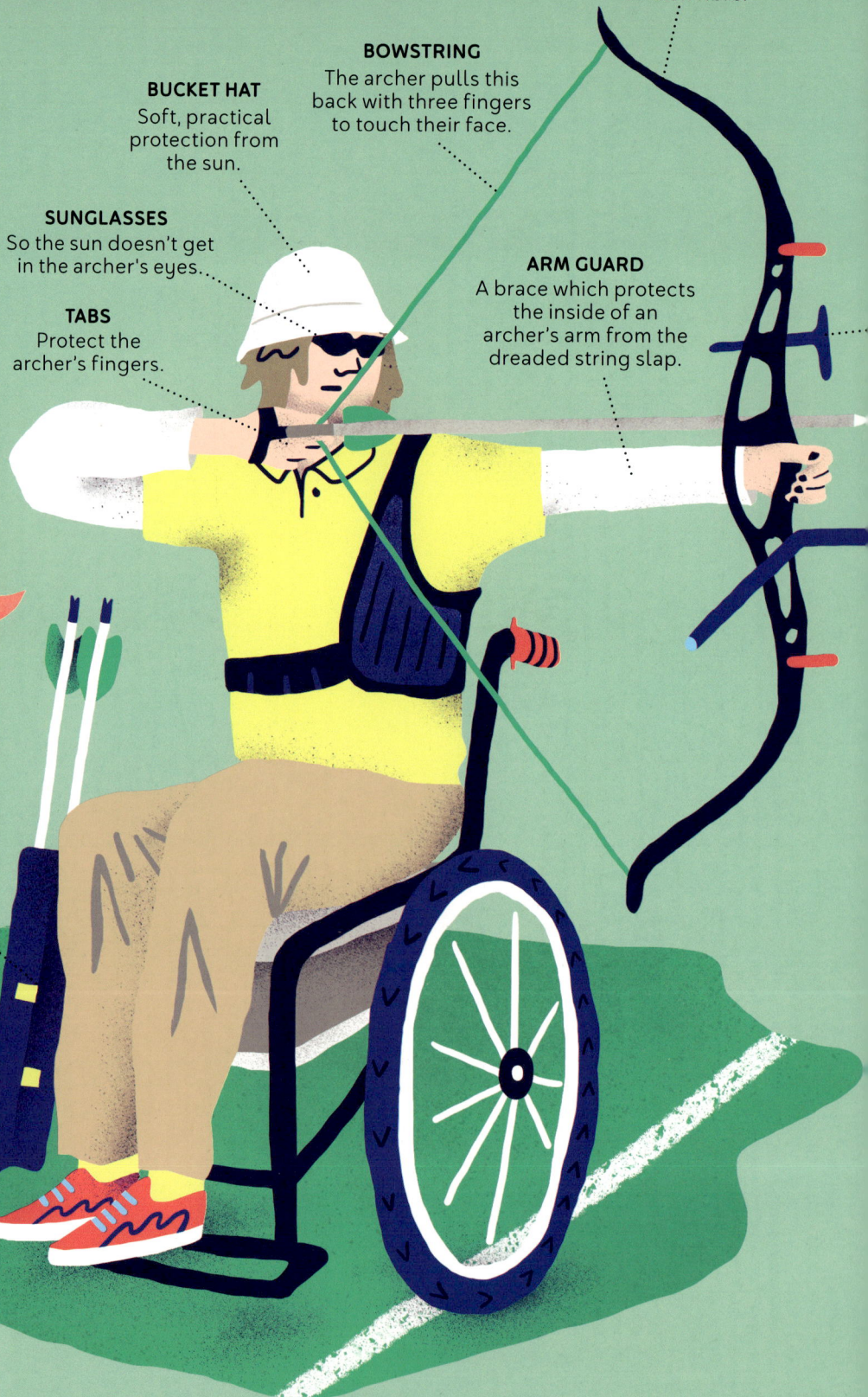

The Rules

Thankfully, in Olympic archery they don't shoot at humans or animals, they aim at a target made up of a series of different coloured rings. The gold inner ring gives you a maximum ten-point score. The top archers in the world hit gold most of the time and get really stroppy if they get a different colour. They do not shout, "it's a bullseye" when they hit it. That happens in darts.

CHANCE OF BECOMING A CHAMPION

Slim | OK | Good ↑ | Great

Nowadays, only about 60,000 people in the UK would describe themselves as archers, so the chances of becoming a champion are high.

The History Bit

People have been using bows since the Stone Age, but mainly for hunting. Fed up with using them just to catch food, the ancient Egyptians turned them into a battlefield weapon and a sport. The first recorded tournament was in China way back in 1027 BCE. So, archery is really, really, really old.

INJURIES

Archery is a relatively safe sport, as it's non-contact and you stand dead still. However, wrist, elbow and shoulder injuries can happen due to the constant force required when pulling back the bowstring. You could get really hurt if you decided to wander about near the targets when people are practising.

SKILLS NEEDED

A good aim, steady arms, mental toughness and loads of patience. You need to be accurate, but also consistent.

SIGHT
A rod with a viewfinder on the end which helps the archer aim at the target, not the crowd.

DISTANCE
Seventy metres — that's about the length of two-and-a-half blue whales. But it's measured with a tape measure, not an actual whale.

TARGET
You want to be hitting the gold centre, every time, for maximum points.

70 METRES

STABILISER
Helps the archer hold the bow still.

BASIC TRAINING

It's easy to set up targets in your garden, but you'll have to get hold of a toy bow that fires plastic or wooden arrows with a rubber stopper. Don't use ones with metal tips — they're deadly weapons.

BEST EVER

The South Koreans are the true Robin Hoods of archery — they hold all the score records across male, female and mixed events, and have won 43 medals, 27 of those being golds. Other countries don't even get close to that medal haul! It's not surprising since children in South Korean primary schools often have two-hour archery lessons as part of their day. Kim Soo-Nyung tops the medal list with six in total, and yes, she's South Korean too.

KIM'S MEDAL COUNT:
🥇 X4   🥈 X1   🥉 X1

UPSIDES

Watching the arrow you've just shot fly through the air and hit a gold target, a long way away, is very satisfying. Plus, you can imagine what it must have been like being an archer back in the Middle Ages.

DOWNSIDES

Releasing an arrow is not as easy as you think. It's tough pulling the string back and when you loose the arrow it can give you a right old whack on the inside of your arm. After all that, you could suddenly realise your arrow has landed in a lake nowhere near the target.

BOXING

WHAT IS IT?

Two fighters stand in a ring, which is actually a square, and bash each other in the face and body until one of them is declared the winner.

The Rules

The rules are constantly changing and there are a lot of them because it's so dangerous, but essentially male boxers fight for three three-minute rounds and female boxers fight for four two-minute rounds. The fighter who lands the most punches on their opponent will win the fight either by a 'knockout', the referee stepping in to stop the fight or the judges' decision.

You can only use your fists to hit your opponent. Elbowing, headbutting, biting and hair-pulling will all result in losing points or disqualification. You also can't punch below the belt.

PROTECTIVE HEADGEAR
Since 2016, men don't have to wear headgear, but women still do.

PLAIN SHORTS
No fancy shiny shorts here . . . just plain red or blue.

SKILLS NEEDED

You need to be tough, fit and not bothered about getting whacked in the face. If you burst into tears when you fall over, stay well clear. Your size doesn't matter as there are different weight divisions with names like flyweight and featherweight. You don't actually have to weigh as much as a fly or a feather. That would be silly.

RING
Boxing started in a chalk circle drawn on the floor. Now it's on a raised square platform, so it's easier to see the fight.

INJURIES

Concussions, brain injuries, broken bones, memory loss . . . the list goes on. Think of an injury and a boxer could get it.

THE HISTORY BIT

Hand-to-hand fighting has been around ever since Caveman Dave took a swing at his neighbour for stealing his wooly mammoth. It's so old the ancient Greeks made it a proper competition in the Olympics in 688 BCE. Boxing has been part of the modern Olympics since 1904, and women's boxing joined in 2012.

CANVAS
Padded floor of the ring, not used for painting.

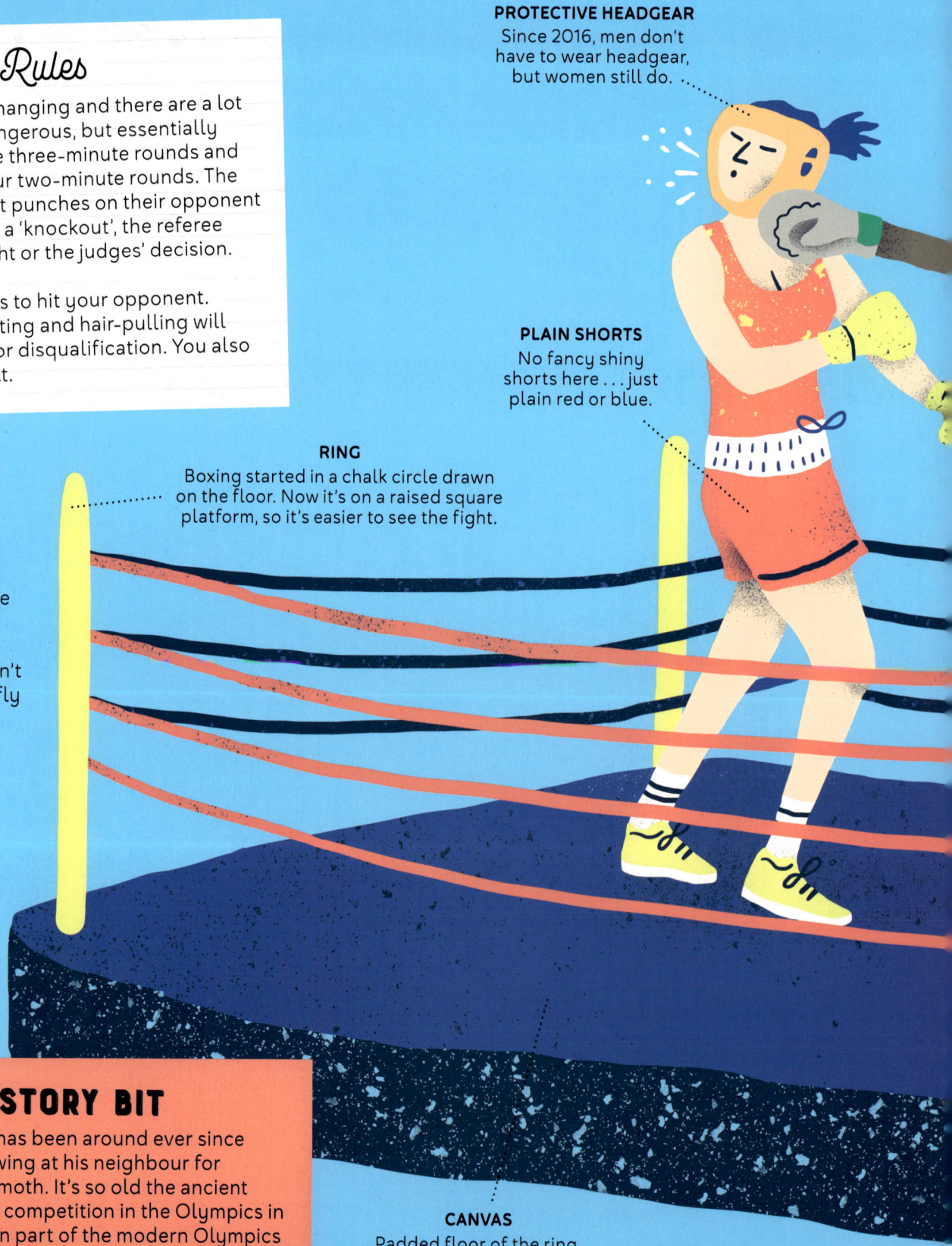

Sound Like a Pro

"BREADBASKET" – Another term for a boxer's stomach.

"GLASS JAW" – A boxer with a weak chin, who gets knocked out a lot.

"RABBIT PUNCH" – An illegal punch to the back of the neck.

"SOUTHPAW" – A left-handed boxer.

"HAYMAKER" – A wild, swinging punch.

CHANCE OF BECOMING A CHAMPION

Slim	OK	Good	Great

Because you get bashed in the face so much, people tend to steer clear of doing it as a job!

BASIC TRAINING

Put on a pair of oven gloves and punch fresh air for ten minutes. If you can do that without feeling tired then you've passed stage one. Now do the same again, but get a friend to clobber you with a pillow, and then go for a 16-kilometre run. You have to do all of this without moaning or losing your temper.

MOUTHGUARD
Like your teeth? This will help keep them in your mouth.

GLOVES
Large, padded leather gloves, usually filled with foam, used to protect the boxer's hands and wrists and the opponent's face . . . sort of.

A CLOSER LOOK

BEST EVER

USA (117 medals) and Cuba (78 medals) are the best boxing nations by far. It's Cuba's best Olympic sport and their stars are Félix Savón and Teófilo Stevenson with three golds each. In women's boxing, Great Britain's Nicola Adams and USA's Claressa Shields have two golds each. Most boxers turn professional after winning just one Olympic medal.

ROPES
To stop the boxers running away. Being 'on the ropes' is not a good thing, as it usually means your opponent is winning.

UPSIDES

Becoming an Olympic champion usually leads on to becoming World Champion and one of the most famous people on the planet. It also means earning loads of money. Even the top professional fighters who get knocked out in the first round can earn millions.

DOWNSIDES

This is obvious. Getting beaten up, and the training is incredibly hard.

FENCING

WHAT IS IT?

Very polite sword fighting in a straight line.
It does not involve putting up a fence.

The Rules

Fencers score points by hitting each other with their
weapon. The one with the most points at the end
of three rounds, or whoever gets to 15 points first,
wins. However, it's not quite that simple. There are
three different types of weapon (all very thin and
long), with different rules for each one. Wheelchair
fencers have a wheelchair that is fixed to the floor,
so their bouts are very fast and tactical.

THE HISTORY BIT

People have been fighting each other
with swords for thousands of years,
but fencing wasn't turned into a proper
sport until the 17th and 18th centuries.
A mask was invented and the weapon's
tip was flattened, because plunging
a sword into someone's chest wasn't
considered very sporting. Fencing
arrived at the Olympics in 1896 and
wheelchair fencing was one of the
sports at the first Paralympics in 1960.

BASIC TRAINING

Get a friend, go to a
wood and find two
long, thin sticks. Lunge
and prance towards
each other with
the very tip of your
wooden sword.

LAMÉ
The electric
scoring jacket
worn on top of
the cotton jacket.

JACKET
Usually made of tough
cotton with a strap that goes
between your legs, to keep
it in place. Probably not as
padded as you'd hope.

LONG SOCKS THAT GO UP TO THE KNEE
This is not a scruffy
sport, so keep
them pulled up.

HAND GUARD
Épées have a
metal guard
to protect the
fencer's fingers.

ÉPEE, FOIL or SABRE
Fencers like to call these thr
types of blade their weapon
but they're actually blunt
and have no sharp edges.
Foils and épées are made fo
moves that use a pointing o
'stabbing' motion, whereas
sabre is made to perform
a 'slashing' motion.

SKILLS NEEDED

You should be handy with a weapon but also nimble on your
feet because there's a lot of prancing back and forward.
Shouting and yelling during the bouts is also a key skill,
mainly to intimidate your opponent, but also to try and
convince a referee that you scored a point.

CHANCE OF BECOMING A CHAMPION

| Slim | OK | Good | ▲ Great |

In most countries, fencing is not
one of the most popular sports.

"EN GARDE" or "ON GUARD"

— Spoken at the start of a duel, to warn your opponent you're about to come at them with a sword.

"APPEL"
— Stamping your front foot to try and put your opponent off.

"DIRECTOR"
— The referee.

"SALLE"
— The room where you do your fencing.

"BLACK CARD"
— The worst type of card in any sport. You've done something really bad if you get one of these and it means immediate expulsion from the tournament.

BEST EVER

Italy and France are the true masters at fencing, with 130 and 123 medals. Hungary are not bad either, with 90 medals.

Edoardo Mangiarotti is the world's most successful fencer, and Italy's best ever Olympian, with a huge 13 medals. He started fencing aged eight and turned himself into a left-handed fencer because they are more difficult to fight against.

MANGIAROTTI'S MEDAL COUNT: 1 X6 2 X5 3 X2

UPSIDES

Successfully hitting someone with your weapon at the same time as they're trying to hit you is a great feeling, especially as it's actually very hard to do.

DOWNSIDES

The equipment is expensive, and everyone will constantly ask you if they can "have a quick go with your sword".

PLASTRON
Protects your chest and underarms

INJURIES

Even though weapons are blunt and you wear protective clothing, a heavy prod in the chest or a whack on the hand can still deliver some belting bruises. It's sword fighting, after all.

BREECHES
These are short trousers held up by braces, sometimes called knickers. It's the only sport where you wear your knickers on the outside.

A CLOSER LOOK

FENCING MASK
This has a mesh front to protect the face, and a bib that protects the neck.

EPIC FAIL

French fencer Enzo Lefort's mobile phone fell out of his back pocket during a match against a German fencer. He went on to lose the bout and he missed the call from his mum asking him what he wanted for his tea.

Judo

WHAT IS IT?

A Japanese martial art where competitors, known as 'judokas', try to throw their opponent to the floor. Judo means the 'gentle way', but hurling your rival over your shoulder is anything but gentle.

SKILLS NEEDED

Judokas can be all shapes and sizes, and competitors are put into different weight divisions. So, if you're really small, you won't be battling against a massive judoka with arms made of steel. Brute strength is not that important, but you will need good balance, courage and cunning.

The Rules

Judokas spend most of each four-minute judo bout seemingly trying to remove each other's jackets. But they are actually trying to throw their opponent on their back or trap them on the floor for 20 seconds, so they can claim something called ippon, which gives you an automatic victory. There are lots of other throws that sound cool, but they're not as powerful as an ippon.

You can't kick or punch or poke your opponent in the face. Hair-pulling, teeth-grabbing and wild screaming are also no-nos. You need to concentrate on throwing, grappling and holding.

For Paralympians, only athletes with sight impairments can compete, and they are divided into sight classes and weight divisions.

HYGIENE

All judokas must have short fingernails and toenails. Long hair must be tied up and competitors must smell fresh. So, make sure you have a shower before a match. Your opponent will win automatically if you turn up looking like you slept in a hedge.

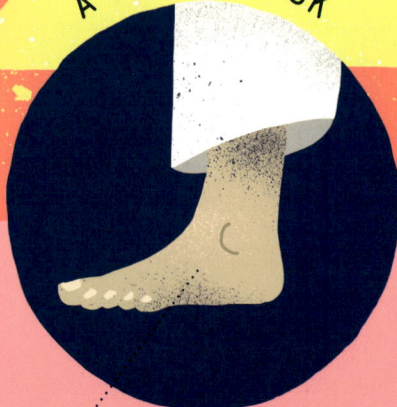

IPPON

Also known as 'the perfect throw'. If you pull this off then you've won automatically.

A BLUE JUDOGI

It's hard to see what is going on when two players wearing white are grappling, so one wears blue instead.

A CLOSER LOOK

BARE FEET

If you struggle doing up your shoelaces, then judo is the perfect sport for you.

THE HISTORY BIT

Judo looks like it should be thousands of years old — something the samurai warriors used to practise when they weren't swirling their swords around — but actually it was only created in 1882. Judo joined the Olympics in 1964, and the 2021 games included a mixed team event for the first time.

BASIC TRAINING

The most important bit of judo is knowing how to fall properly. There are several fall-breaking techniques called ukemi. A bed is the perfect place to practise falling – just make sure that no one is asleep in it first!

INJURIES

Back, shoulder and knee injuries are most common. However, judo legend Yasuhiro Yamashita won gold in the 1984 Olympics despite tearing a calf muscle in the quarter finals!

"O-GOSHI"
oh-gosh-shee
– A powerful hip throw.

"WAZA-ARI"
wah-zah-ah-ree
– The second highest score in judo, after an ippon.

"KARI-ASHI"
kah-ree-ah-shee
– A foot sweep.

"MAITTA"
mah-ee-tah
– The signal, made by tapping the mat twice, that a judoka is giving up the bout.

"MATE"
mah-tay
– Means wait. The referee calls this if they spot a problem, usually to get judokas to fix their gi.

BEST EVER

French heavyweight Teddy Riner has five medals, including three gold won at consecutive Olympics. Japan's Tadahiro Nomura also has three golds. Ryoko Tani has five Olympic medals, two gold, two silver and a bronze and she's also won seven world titles. Unsurprisingly, as the inventor of judo, Japan dominates the medal table with 96, including 48 gold.

RINER'S MEDAL COUNT:

🥇 X3   🥉 X2

A THICK COTTON JACKET AND TROUSERS CALLED A JUDOGI OR GI

The gi is tied round the waist by a coloured belt, or 'obi', that shows how good you are.

REFEREE

A smartly dressed person who strolls around the judokas and makes hand gestures to award points or penalties.

PROTECTIVE MATS CALLED TATAMI

These soft mats stop your bones from shattering into a thousand pieces.

UPSIDES

You don't have to be stacked with muscles to be a top judoka, plus there are some awesome takedowns in judo.

DOWNSIDES

Some people don't like being tossed in the air or trimming their toenails.

CHANCE OF BECOMING A CHAMPION

Slim — OK — Good — Great

Over 40 million people around the world practise judo, but your chances are even slimmer if you are from Asia or France, since that's usually where the best judokas come from.

WRESTLING

WHAT IS IT?

A combat sport where two athletes in singlets roll around on a mat cuddling each other until one of them can't move any more.

The Rules

There are two types of wrestling at the Olympics – Greco-Roman and freestyle. Greco-Roman is only for men and allows you to attack only above the waist, with your upper body or arms. In freestyle, pretty much anything goes!

Your main aim is to pin your opponent's shoulders to the mat for one second, called a fall. You also get bonus points for holds and throws through the bout.

Matches are two periods of three minutes, but each ends if there's a fall or a difference of ten points (freestyle) or eight points (Greco-Roma n). You can also win if your opponent gets three warnings for foul play or for being too defensive, also known as being boring.

THE HISTORY BIT

Wrestling is one of the oldest Olympic sports, first performed in the ancient Olympics, when nobody wore any clothes. For the next couple of thousand years, various civilisations invented their own versions of wrestling and now it's done by most children, and some adults, when they're arguing over who gets the TV remote control.

Wrestling joined the Olympics in 1896, but women's wrestling only appeared in 2004.

BEST EVER

USA have the most combined wrestling medals, with Russia, Japan, Sweden, Bulgaria and Turkey ranking highly. Japan's Kaori Icho and Cuba's Mijaín López are the best Olympic freestyle wrestlers with four gold medals each.

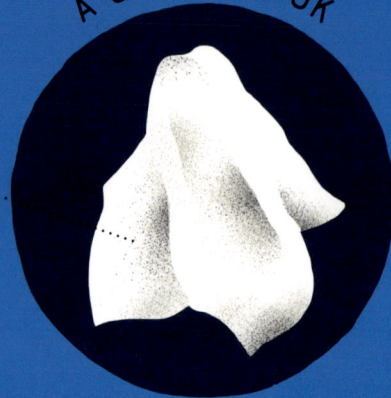

A WHITE HANDKERCHIEF
This is used for quickly wiping away any blood or snot and you get a warning if you don't carry one at all times.

A CLOSER LOOK

SKILLS NEEDED

You need to be strong and powerful with a quick-thinking, strategic mind to spot the opportunity to strike. Stay clear if you don't like getting really close to someone's armpit.

REFEREE
The referee awards points, uses a whistle to start and stop the action and is helped out by a judge and a mat chairman who sit off the mat.

MAT
A circular, thick rubber mat, a bit like a giant marshmallow.

Slim	OK	Good	↑	Great

Wrestling is very popular in Turkey, Mongolia and the countries that surround Russia. However, because of the popularity of professional wrestling, like WWE, it is now considered to be a dying art. So, this is your chance. What are you waiting for?

Sound Like a Pro

"SQUEEEEEZE" – The crowd shouts this to encourage the wrestler on top to hold on to the wrestler who is trying to escape.

"FIVE" – Throwing an opponent head over feet, which gets you five points.

"TAKEDOWN" – When you take your opponent down to the mat and gain control.

"CAULIFLOWER EAR" – When your ear gets all lumpy due to constant bashing.

SLIPPERY GRIP
Covering yourself in grease, so you can slip out of your opponent's grip, is banned.

SHOOTING SLEEVE
Thinner than a knee pad, this helps wrestlers slide over the mat.

SHORT NAILS
So you can't slice your opponent.

GUMSHIELD
Like your smile? Wear one of these.

SINGLET
One contestant wears red, the other wears blue.

KNEE PADS
Protect against knee injuries, especially as you spend a lot of time crouched or on the floor.

WRESTLING SHOES
These are the only required piece of equipment, but to keep everyone from laughing, you might want to buy a singlet too.

BASIC TRAINING

A younger brother or sister can be your perfect training partner. Create a totally unnecessary argument, like 'who gets the last good cereal from the selection pack', and then wrestle for it until you've managed to get both their shoulders on the carpet. Remove the cereal from their hand, eat it, then get your mum to flap a tea towel at you to cool you down — wrestling is a very sweaty business.

UPSIDES

Battling your opponent, tactically out-thinking them and then throwing or pinning them to the floor is the ultimate form of battle chess.

DOWNSIDES

If you don't like getting your face smooshed into the floor or covered in someone else's sweat, stay on the sofa.

INJURIES

You name it and you'll get it in wrestling. Bruises, sprains, cuts, fractures and concussions — wrestling has them all.

TAEKWONDO

WHAT IS IT?

A combat sport where two fighters try to kick or punch each other in the body or head to score points.

The Rules

There are three two-minute rounds, with a minute's break in between, when coaches get to flap a towel in your face to cool you down. Judges award points for the more exciting kicks and punches — a normal body blow gets one point, a kick to the head gets two and knocking down an opponent gets three. Plus, you get an extra point for doing any of these moves while spinning.

Points are taken away for fouls like attacking the face, punching the head, pulling your opponent to the ground, stepping over the mat boundary and turning your back on your opponent.

The athlete with either a knockdown or the most points at the end of three rounds wins.

BASIC TRAINING

Do lots of stretches to warm up, then put a balloon on the roof of your dad's car and see if you can leap up, spin and kick it off. If you smash the windows, one of the wing mirrors or put a big dent in the door, run and hide under your bed for three months until he has calmed down.

A CLOSER LOOK

HEADGEAR
As kicks to the head are one of the main moves, protective headgear is an important bit of kit.

PROTECTIVE CLOTHING
Athletes wear headgear, a gumshield, arm and shin pads, and body and groin protectors.

DOBOK
A white V-neck jacket and loose trousers.

HOGU
Padded chest protector in red or blue that fits over the shoulders and is laced together at the back. This is the most common scoring zone.

ELECTRONIC SOCKS
Sensors in the socks help record the kicks' accuracy and power. Don't put them in the washing machine.

INJURIES

Even with all the padding, taekwondo can still hurt sometimes. The most common injuries are muscle strains, but kicks to the head can lead to neck injuries and concussions.

EPIC FAILS

Cuban athlete Ángel Matos was so angry at being disqualified from the bronze medal match at the 2008 Olympics he kicked the Swedish referee in the face. Matos, who had won gold at the 2000 Olympics, was banned from the sport for life.

"KYUNGNET"
kyong-nyeh
– Bow. Make sure you do this before every fight.

"KIHAP"
kee-ahp
– Shout this when kicking or punching with power.

"SHI-JAK!"
tshee-jahg
– Referees shout this to start the bout.

"CHAGI"
chah-gee
– Kick.

The History Bit

Taekwondo was developed after the Second World War by Korean martial arts masters. *Tae* means 'foot', *kwon* means 'fist' and *do* means 'way of', so taekwondo means 'the way of the foot and fist' or 'the way of kicking and punching'. It's now practised in almost 200 countries across the globe and became an Olympic sport in 2000 and a Paralympic sport in 2021.

CHANCE OF BECOMING A CHAMPION

| Slim | OK | Good | Great |

Each country is allowed to enter only one athlete per weight category, so basically, you need to be the best fighter in your whole country. But it is a growing sport, so if you get involved now, you could have a chance.

0:17

0 - 0

SKILLS NEEDED

You need to be brave, strong, stretchy and agile to become a good taekwondo fighter. If you can't touch your toes or lift your leg easily on to the kitchen table, then a flying spinning kick will be impossible. You don't need to be bursting with muscles, as male and female athletes are put into weight categories – fly, feather, middleweight and heavyweight.

COLOURED BELT
You'll have to have a black belt or above to compete in the Olympics. The more markings you have on your black belt, the higher your rank.

MAT
Matches are fought on an 8-metre-diameter octagonal mat.

BEST EVER

South Korea, where the sport was invented, has the most medals with 22, 12 of those gold. But watch out for China (11) and USA (10) sneaking up in second and third.

USA's Steven López and Iran's Hadi Saei have three medals each, both with two golds. South Korea's Hwan Kyung-Seon is the first woman to win three Olympic taekwondo medals, two gold and one bronze.

UPSIDES

Taekwondo is fast, furious and great to watch. It rewards attacking shots, so athletes are always looking to pull off the spinning head kick.

DOWNSIDES

It takes a lot of work to learn all the moves and get them right.

HWAN'S MEDAL COUNT: 1 X2 3 X1

Aquatics

SWIMMING

WHAT IS IT?

Travelling up and down a massive rectangular pool of water as fast as you can, by waving your arms and legs about in four different styles.

The Rules

Swim faster than everyone else until you reach the finish.

SHORTS CALLED JAMMERS FOR MEN
Torsos and lower legs must remain bare.

A ONE-PIECE SWIMSUIT FOR WOMEN
These are made from a high-tech material that reduces drag in the water.

EARPLUGS
Some swimmers wear plugs in their ears to stop water getting in.

STARTING BLOCK
Some races start with swimmers diving in from a little platform above their lane.

LANE ROPES
The pool is split into lanes by ropes, held up by plastic floaters, stretched between each end.

NO ASSISTANCE
Paralympic swimmers are not allowed prostheses or assistive devices to help them in the pool, so these need to be removed before they jump in.

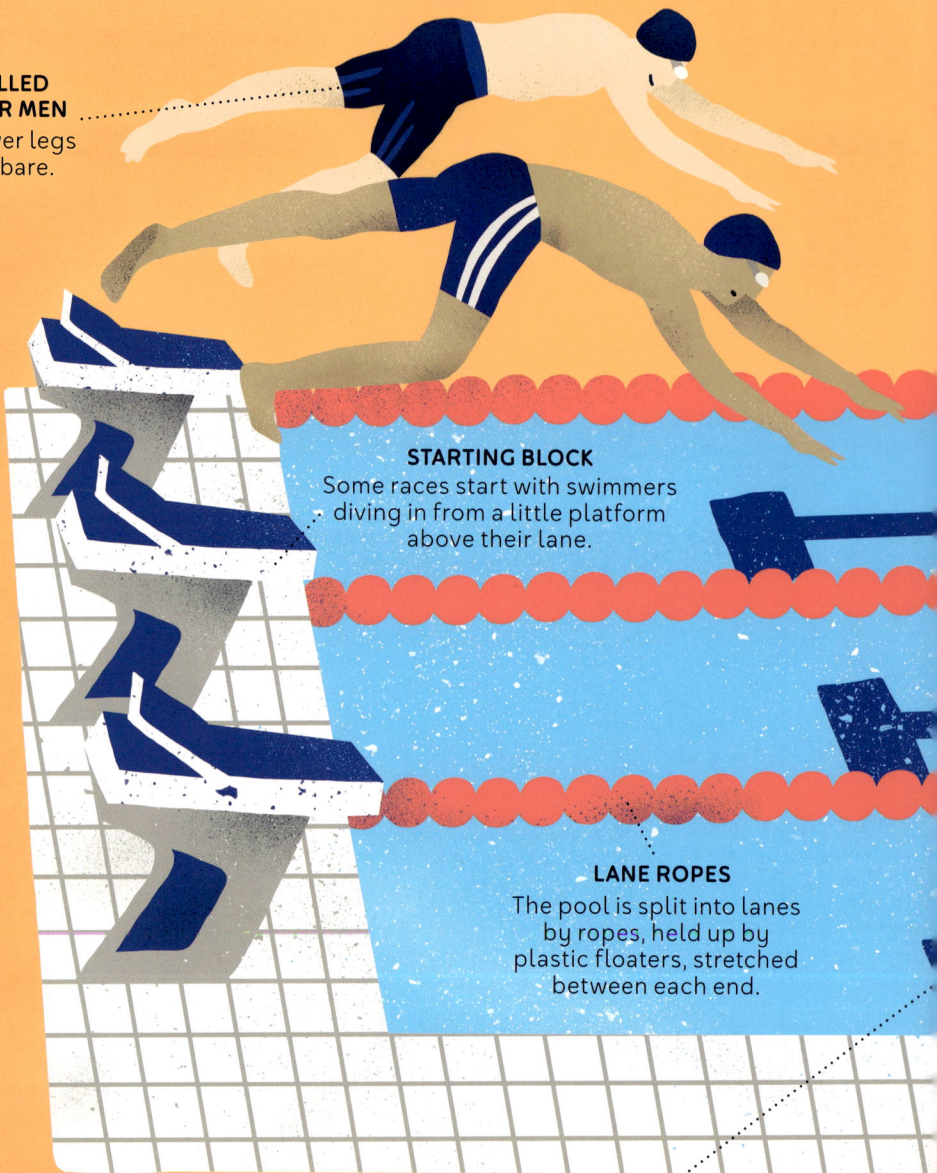

LINES
Straight lines on the bottom of the pool help swimmers stay in the middle of their lane, while T-shapes let them know they're coming to the end of the pool.

THE EVENTS

BREASTSTROKE

This is the slowest stroke. To do breaststroke, you need to perfect your frog-leg kicks and imagine your hands are scooping out a bowl of porridge and then throwing it behind you.

FREESTYLE

You can do any stroke you like in freestyle, but so far nobody has won a medal doing the doggy-paddle. Front crawl is the fastest stroke and swimmers hardly take a breath.

BACKSTROKE

Backstroke is swimming on your back, with your arms going round and round like a windmill.

BUTTERFLY

This is the most exhausting and difficult stroke, with a great deal of splashing from both your arms and legs.

UPSIDES

It has low impact on the body and is great for keeping fit. Pools are nice and warm and it's great if you need a wash.

DOWNSIDES

Early morning starts. Most wannabe top swimmers are still at school so they have to start training before lessons. Also, your career is short, as swimmers usually retire in their twenties.

The History Bit

Swimming was invented by people in the Stone Age after they discovered that too many of them were drowning when they tried to walk underwater.

Despite having been around for thousands of years, swimming didn't become a racing sport until the 19th century. It was at the Olympics in 1896 and the first Paralympics in 1960. Just to be different, backstroke didn't join until 1904 and women's swimming joined in 1912.

NO HAIR ON YOUR BODY

You are basically trying to make yourself as smooth and slippery as possible, like a bar of soap in the bath or a dolphin.

A CLOSER LOOK

BASIC TRAINING

Fill a sink with water and dunk your head into it. After about ten seconds, turn your head to the side, so your mouth is out of the water, and take a gulp of air. Do this until your mum tells you off for splashing water all over the floor.

GOGGLES AND CAP

Caps aren't compulsory, but most swimmers wear them. Plastic goggles help swimmers see underwater and protect their eyes from stinging chemicals.

SKILLS NEEDED

It helps to have long arms, long legs, big feet and big lungs.

Sound Like a Pro

"TUMBLE TURN"
— An underwater somersault done at the end of a length to turn around quickly.

"PB"
— Personal best for a stroke and distance.

"OPEN TURN"
— A two-handed touch turn used in breaststroke and butterfly.

"DOLPHIN KICK"
— Whipping your legs while keeping your feet together, used in butterfly.

BEST EVER

USA has a massive haul of 579 Olympic medals, 257 of those gold, and 722 medals earned at the Paralympics. That's a lot of medals!

Michael Phelps is the king of the swimmers and the most successful Olympic athlete ever. His nicknames are the 'Flying Fish' and the 'Baltimore Bullet'. . . because he comes from Baltimore and swims as fast as a bullet.

American Paralympic swimmer Trischa Zorn has 55 medals and is the most successful Paralympian of all time.

ZORN'S MEDAL COUNT: 1 X41   2 X9   3 X5

INJURIES

It's very hard to break a bone in the water, so swimmers mostly get muscle injuries. However, if you choose the backstroke, you will probably bash your head on the wall a few times. So, expect a bruised head.

CHANCE OF BECOMING A CHAMPION

Slim	OK	Good	Great

Low because swimming is very popular across the world and an essential life skill.

AQUATICS
Diving

WHAT IS IT?

Leaping off a high board, performing a series of elaborate acrobatics, then landing perfectly in the pool without making a big splash.

The Rules

Diving is very simple. You dive a number of times to score as many points as possible. The diver with the most points wins. The scoring is where it gets tricky as it's based on factors including difficulty of the dive, take-off and splash, and points are deducted from a perfect score of 10. So, just turning up and doing a massive bomb won't win you any medals.

THE HISTORY BIT

People have been jumping off cliffs to prove how tough they are since ancient times. However, it didn't turn into a competition until the 1880s. Various forms of diving (plain, fancy and highboard) started appearing in the Olympics in the early 1900s, but the types of diving we see today (springboard and platform) didn't join until 1928. Synchronised diving, where two people dive at the same time, joined in 2000.

A CLOSER LOOK

SHAMMY
No diver should be without a tiny towel for staying dry between dives.

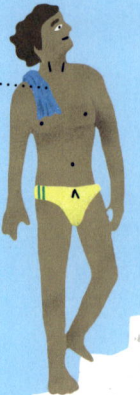

SWIMMING BRIEFS
The smaller, the better. Female divers wear a one-piece swimsuit.

3-METRE SPRINGBOARD
A super-springy board used for bouncing as high as you can to pull off awesome acrobatics in the air.

BASIC TRAINING

You'll have to go to your local pool that has a diving board. If you're feeling brave, climb to the top and peer over the edge. If your legs don't turn to jelly, jump off the top, feet first. If that wasn't too bad, do it again and again . . .

UPSIDES

Diving is one of the most popular spectator sports at the Olympics and if you get it right, it looks very impressive.

DOWNSIDES

The fear factor is huge. Getting your dive wrong and smacking into the water can also make you look a bit silly, and it hurts.

"SMACK"
— Hitting the water at the wrong angle. Ouch!

"RIP"
— When a diver enters the water vertically with hardly any splash.

"BAIL"
— When a diver pulls out of the move in mid-air, usually ending with a smack.

INJURIES

Despite it looking dangerous, nasty diving injuries are quite rare. But bruising from bad smacks, and shoulder, back and arm injuries can happen.

10-METRE PLATFORM

As high as two giraffes — one standing on top of the other. Giraffes only stand on each other's shoulders when humans are not looking.

BEST EVER

USA have the most medals with a whopping 141, including 49 gold! However, in recent years China has started to dominate, especially in women's diving. They now have 47 golds in their pile of 81 medals. China's Wu Minxia is the most decorated Olympic diver with seven medals, five gold.

WU'S MEDAL COUNT: 1 X5   2 X1   3 X1

PIKE POSITION

When the diver bends their body at the waist, with straight legs and pointed toes. Nothing like the fish.

EPIC WIN

American diver Greg Louganis cracked his head on the board at the start of one of his dives at the 1988 Olympics. He got a concussion but still went on to win gold!

CHANCE OF BECOMING A CHAMPION

Slim | OK | Good | Great

Diving is not a common sport in schools even though some Olympic divers are as young as 14. People usually start with gymnastics or trampolining before moving to the diving pit if they're brave enough.

REALLY DEEP POOL

To make diving safe, there is a deep pool called a pit or a well underneath the boards. To make it even safer, sharks don't live in the pool.

SKILLS NEEDED

The most important thing is bravery. If you conquer the high board and leap off the top, you'll be travelling towards the water at around 40 kilometres per hour. That's seriously scary.

You also need to be good at gymnastics, acrobatics or dancing. Some dives even start with a handstand, so get practising.

AQUATICS
WATER POLO

WHAT IS IT?

A team sport where you throw a ball around a swimming pool to try and score as many goals as possible.

Sound Like a Pro

"SKIP SHOT"
— A powerful shot aimed into the water, so it hopefully skips across the pool and into the goal.

"DRY PASS"
— A pass thrown and caught without the ball touching the water.

"TANK"
— Another name for the pool.

"DONUT"
— A goal scored over the goalie's head and through their outstretched arms.

"CHERRY PICKING" or **"SEAGULLING"**
— When the defending team leaves one player in an attacking position, waiting to strike on goal.

BASIC TRAINING

Go to your nearest swimming pool and tread water for 30 minutes without touching the sides. Then get a friend to tackle you underwater as you try and throw a ball one-handed to the other end of the pool. Easy!

The Rules

Two teams of seven (including a goalie) have to score the most goals by throwing a ball into their opponents' net using only one hand. Only the goalie can use two hands. There are loads of fouls in water polo — one is even called a brutality — and players who commit fouls spend time in a 'sin-bin'.

A match is four quarters of eight minutes, but they can go on for much longer as the clock is stopped when the ball is not in play. Teams only get 30 seconds for each attack.

SWIMMING POOL
The pool is all deep end, so you can't touch the bottom. It's usually 20–30 metres long and 10–20 metres wide, with floating goals 3 metres wide and 0.9 metres tall.

GUMSHIELD
Water polo can be very violent and you need your teeth to eat afterwards.

TIGHT, LIGHT SWIMSUITS
Suit-grabbing fouls are common, so swimsuits need to be tough.

THE HISTORY BIT

Water polo began in Britain in the mid-1800s as rugby in water. It was basically two teams beating each other up in a river or a lake as they tried to get a rubber ball to the other side. Players would hide the ball in their swimsuits, dunk other players' heads underwater and wrestle. It was mayhem until the introduction of stricter rules at the 1900 Olympics. Women's water polo was added 100 years later.

SKILLS NEEDED
You need to be a strong swimmer who is very good at treading water and doesn't mind getting splashed and bashed up.

A CLOSER LOOK

SWIMMING CAP
This has your number on it to show your position.

GOALIE'S CAP
A different colour to the rest of their team.

EAR PROTECTORS
To stop your ears getting torn off and to keep water out.

UPSIDES
You don't have to swim in a boring straight line, like in swimming. Water polo is fast and furious.

DOWNSIDES
Most top players are really muscly, so getting bashed about will hurt.

INJURIES
A ball in the face, battered ears, nail scratches, swallowing loads of pool water and itchy eyes because water polo players don't wear goggles!

BEST EVER
Hungary reigns supreme with 16 medals, nine gold. USA tops the medal table in the women's event with three golds out of six medals.

CHANCE OF BECOMING A CHAMPION

Slim   OK   Good   Great

If you live in Africa or Asia, your chances are very high. Countries in these continents have never won a medal and sometimes don't even bother entering. Your chances are slimmer if you live in Eastern Europe because water polo is a big deal there.

AQUATICS

Artistic Swimming

WHAT IS IT?

Gymnastics and ballet in a swimming pool, in sparkly costumes, set to music. It used to be called synchronised swimming, but they changed the name to try to increase the sport's popularity.

A SPARKLY COSTUME
Swimmers wear beautifully decorated swimsuits to match their beautiful choreography. Male swimmers wear sparkly swim shorts.

HAIR GEL
Swimmers use gel to plaster their hair to their head so it doesn't move during their performance.

NO TOUCHING THE BOTTOM
This makes all the lifts even more impressive.

NO GOGGLES
So you can make eye contact with the judges at all times.

INJURIES
It's mainly back and hip injuries from all the dance moves, plus you'll probably swallow a lot of water.

LOTS OF DIFFERENT FACIAL EXPRESSIONS
The 'grinning like a monkey that has just pinched the last bag of crisps' seems to be the most popular.

The History Bit

Everyone tries to do a handstand underwater when they are on holiday. But rather than just getting a round of applause from their mum, in the early 20th century some people got all fancy with their moves and called it water ballet. They went around performing elaborate routines in shows and films.

A sport was then developed which joined the Olympics as synchronised swimming in 1984.

NOSE CLIP
Swimmers can stay underwater for a really long time thanks to a special clip that stops water going up their nose.

MALE SWIMMERS
Up to two male competitors per artistic swimming team are allowed in the Paris 2024 Olympics — the first time ever male swimmers are allowed to compete in the sport at this level!

48

The Rules

Artistic swimmers perform entertaining routines to music, with moves judged both below and above the water.

There are two events — a duet event, with two swimmers, and a team event, with eight. Each event involves two routines — a technical routine, which lasts just under three minutes, and a free routine, which lasts three to four minutes. Sadly, nobody has tried just mucking about on a lilo, which is a big shame.

Judges score routines on a scale of 100. They look at how synchronised the moves are, how hard the tricks are and at the routine's overall artistic impression.

BEST EVER

Russia have been the rulers of the pool since the 2000s with ten gold medals, and another two under the guise of the Russian Olympic Committee in 2021 (that's a long story). Japan has the most medals with 14, but none of them are gold. Russian Svetlana Romashina has won seven gold medals at four consecutive Olympics and is probably part mermaid.

BASIC TRAINING

Get in the bath with your brother or sister and copy each other's movements for three minutes. Then perform your routine in front of your mum and dad while giving the biggest smile you can smile. If they don't like it, splash them.

UPSIDES

Artistic swimming looks spectacular. Considering most people can't remember what they ate for breakfast, these swimmers have to remember and time their complicated routines perfectly, while spending most of the time underwater holding their breath. Amazing skills.

DOWNSIDES

There's a lot of training and the added pressure of knowing that one mistake could muck up the routine for everyone else. You also have to spend hours in the pool getting very close to your teammates' feet and probably getting wrinkly skin.

A CLOSER LOOK

LOTS OF WATERPROOF MAKE-UP AND DECORATIVE HAIR CLIPS

Artistic swimmers wear heavy theatrical make-up so the judges can see their expressions from far away.

UNDERWATER MUSIC

A speaker under the water helps the swimmers keep in time with the music.

SKILLS NEEDED

You need to be flexible and strong, with great musical timing and good gymnastic ability. It helps to have lungs the size of a whale. Oh, and being a good swimmer is pretty essential.

Sound Like a Pro

"BOOST" — A fast head-first leap out of the water.

"SCULLING" — Hand movements that help balance.

"EGGBEATER" — Treading water by rotating your legs in different directions.

"DECKWORK" — The dance moves performed before getting into the water.

CHANCE OF BECOMING A CHAMPION

Slim — OK — Good — Great

If you're a mermaid, you've got a great chance of winning a medal.

CANOE

WHAT IS IT?

Paddling a thin, pointy boat as fast as you can to beat the other people in the race. Olympic canoeing includes sprint and slalom racing in both canoe and kayak.

THE HISTORY BIT

The canoe is the oldest boat around, as they've been going since prehistoric times. However, people used canoes for transport and hunting rather than racing down rapids with someone timing them, especially as cavemen didn't have stopwatches. Canoe joined the Olympics in 1936 and the Paralympics in 2016.

The Rules

Canoe and kayak sprint couldn't be simpler. It's a straight race to the finish line on a flat stretch of water. Remember, sit down in a kayak and kneel in a canoe.

Slalom is much trickier. You have to weave your way down white-water rapids to get to the finish line, without touching the gates as you pass. To make it even harder, some of the gates are 'upstream', so you have to paddle back up the rapids. Penalty time is added if you touch the gates, miss them completely or go through them backwards. The paddler with the fastest time wins.

SKILLS NEEDED

It's all about upper-body strength. Sprinters need loads of stamina too, especially over the longer distances. You also need great skill and balance to keep your canoe or kayak from flipping over and throwing you out.

A CLOSER LOOK

BUOYANCY AID
Only the slalom Olympians need one of these to keep them afloat if they get thrown into the rapids.

INJURIES

Shoulder and wrist injuries are most common, and you'll also swallow a lot of water.

CANOE PADDLE
These are single-blade, with a T-shaped handle.

CANOE
An open-top boat for one or more paddlers, who fully kneel in slalom or kneel on one knee in sprint.

Hungary is top of the medal table with 86 medals, followed by Germany with 77 (although Germany have the most golds with 34). The best paddler is Germany's Birgit Fischer, who has won 12 medals over six Olympics. She won her first medal when she was 18 and her last aged 42!

FISCHER'S MEDAL COUNT:

🥇 x8   🥈 x4

BASIC TRAINING

Fill up your bath and get in wearing all of your clothes. Pick the biggest spoon you can find in the kitchen, plunge it into the water and do a stroke on the left then a stroke on the right until you get really tired.

KAYAK PADDLE
This is double-bladed and longer than a canoe paddle.

HELMET
Protects your head as you're twisting and turning through all the gates.

KAYAK
A closed-top boat for one or more paddlers, who sit on the floor with their legs stretched out in front of them.

COCKPIT COVER OR SPRAYDECK
This stops water coming into the kayak.

GATES
Paddlers must go upstream through some hanging gates and downstream through others.

UPSIDES

Zipping through the water at high speed or testing yourself against powerful rapids is very exhilarating. If you're in a boat with two or four paddlers it can be a great team sport too.

DOWNSIDES

If you don't like getting wet, then you'll be much happier watching from the riverbank.

Sound Like a Pro

"CAPSIZE"
– When your boat flips over.

"SWAMP"
– When the kayak fills with water accidentally.

"EDDY"
– A circular current of water, like a small whirlpool, that can cause kayaks to flip over.

CHANCE OF BECOMING A CHAMPION

Slim | OK | Good | Great

Not many people own a boat or live near rapids.

SURFING

A CLOSER LOOK

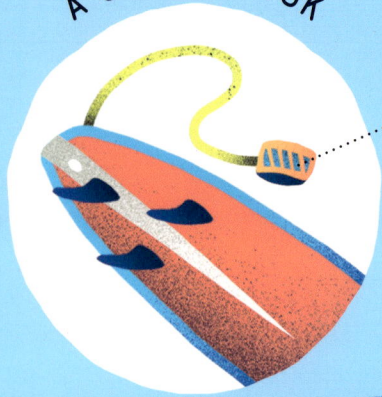

LEASH
Ties around your ankle or wrist and stop the board escaping after you fall off.

WHAT IS IT?

Riding a pointy board on a huge wave while trying to look incredibly cool.

SUN CREAM
Important to protect surfers from the harsh sun.

HAIR CARE
Don't spend hours on your hair before you go surfing as it's going to get very wet.

BOARD WAX
This looks like white chocolate (but don't eat it – it's not very nice). It's rubbed all over the board to give surfers more grip.

CRUNCHER
A massive wave that is really hard to ride.

The Rules

Surfers compete in groups of four and get around 20 minutes to ride any of the waves that the sea throws up. Judges will mark the surfers on the type and difficulty of moves that they do and the two with the highest scores go through to the next round.

Each wave must have only one surfer on it at any time, so there are some polite rules to learn. You'll also have to know which waves look like really good ones, otherwise you'll just end up sitting about with fish nibbling your toes as they dangle in the water.

THE HISTORY BIT

Surfing is thousands of years old. People in the Pacific Ocean islands used boards to ride the waves to quickly get their fishing catches back to shore. European explorers, travellers and tourists noticed the islanders having a great time on their boards and brought the sport back home with them. It started taking off in the late 19th and early 20th centuries.

INJURIES

Falling into water doesn't usually hurt, does it? It does when there's a massive wave crashing down on you. Surfing is dangerous and big cuts, head injuries, concussions, shoulder injuries and bruising are common. Shark bites are very rare, unless you're a character in a film.

BASIC TRAINING

Don't get in the water. Put an ironing board on the floor and lie on top of it. Then practise jumping up on it – this is called a pop-up. It's a bit like a mini press-up. Do this for about an hour. Once you're standing on the board, get someone to try and tip you off it by vigorously rocking the board to and fro.

Sound Like a Pro

"AMPED"
– Excited.

"GOOFY"
– A surfer who rides with his right foot forward.

"WEDGE"
– A really steep wave.

"GROMMET"
– A young surfer.

"STICK"
– Another name for a surfboard.

"SHAKA"
– A hand gesture with your little finger and thumb sticking out. It means lots of things like 'hello', 'cool', 'OK' or 'hang loose'.

"WIPEOUT"
– Falling off the board, usually head-first in a spectacular fashion.

SURF STABILISERS
Fins underneath the board to keep it steady on the wave.

WETSUIT
Surfers wear special suits to keep them warm in the water.

BEST EVER

The Hawaiian Olympic gold medalist swimmer Duke Kahanamoku campaigned through his life to make surfing an Olympic sport. Sadly, it would be over 50 years after his death before it made its Olympic debut in 2021. Brazil's Italo Ferreira and USA's Carissa Moore won the first ever surfing medals.

LIGHTWEIGHT SURFBOARD
A shortboard made of fibreglass, with a pointy end to make it easier to move around.

SOUP
Foam or white water from a broken wave.

SKILLS NEEDED

You'll need balance, strength and the ability to handle lots of salty water smashing into your face, mouth and up your nose.

UPSIDES

Riding a huge wave is a massive thrill and you'll look like the coolest person on the planet.

DOWNSIDES

Falling in lots, swallowing lots of water, calm weather with no waves. Sharks!

CHANCE OF BECOMING A CHAMPION

Slim	OK	Good	Great

There are not many places available in surfing competitions, so you need to be really good.

Rowing

WHAT IS IT?

Facing backwards and using big sticks, or oars, athletes power a long, thin boat across a flat bit of water towards a finish line as fast as they possibly can.

THIN RACING BOAT
The length of the boat depends on how many teammates you have. This can range from two to nine and sometimes rowers compete on their own.

SLIDING SEATS
They go backwards and forwards when you row.

SIMPLE CLOTHING
Some shorts, a singlet and maybe a cap or some sunglasses.

BOW
Usually the smallest in the boat, the bow is responsible for stability, direction and shouting things like, "The other boats are coming!"

OARLOCK
Helps to keep the oars in place.

A MASSIVE OAR
Oars can be more than twice as tall as the rowers. Rowers use one oar for sweeping and two for sculling.

INJURIES
Shoulder, back and forearm injuries are the most common, but you'll get blisters on your hands and feet too.

Skills Needed

Rowers are usually tall, strong and incredibly fit and powerful, with tanks of stamina. There's still a place for you in a rowing crew if you're small though — as a cox. However, you need to be loud and good at leading a boat full of huge rowers.

BASIC TRAINING

Sit on your kitchen floor with a broom in your hands at a right angle. Then lean forwards and backwards moving the stick up and down the floor until you're sweaty and out of breath. Make sure you get someone to splash you with water and shout orders as you are kitchen-rowing. When you've finished, ask your mum for some extra pocket money for sweeping the floor.

THE HISTORY BIT

Rowing is a very old form of transport, popular with the ancient Egyptians, Romans and Greeks. The British turned it into a racing sport in the 1600s and it grew from there, especially in English schools and universities, with the first Oxford v Cambridge boat race in 1829.

Rowing featured in the 1896 Olympics, but the event was called off due to bad weather and a stormy sea. They don't usually row in the sea nowadays because it is too unpredictable.

Women's rowing didn't join the Olympics until 1976, and it didn't feature at the Paralympics until 2008.

SHOES
These come clipped into the boat on a metal plate. Hooray, free shoes!

The Rules

It sounds very simple — row your boat down a 2,000-metre course in a straight line faster than your opponents. However, it's a bit more complicated than that.

You and your teammates have to move the oars in and out of the water with perfect timing or the boat will slow down. So, you can't stop for a second to scratch your nose.

Steering the boat is usually done by one of the rowers, but bigger boats have a small, shouty person sitting at the back, facing the opposite way, called a coxswain, or cox. They control the rudder and bark orders like, "Hurry up, we're losing," and, "My dinner is getting cold."

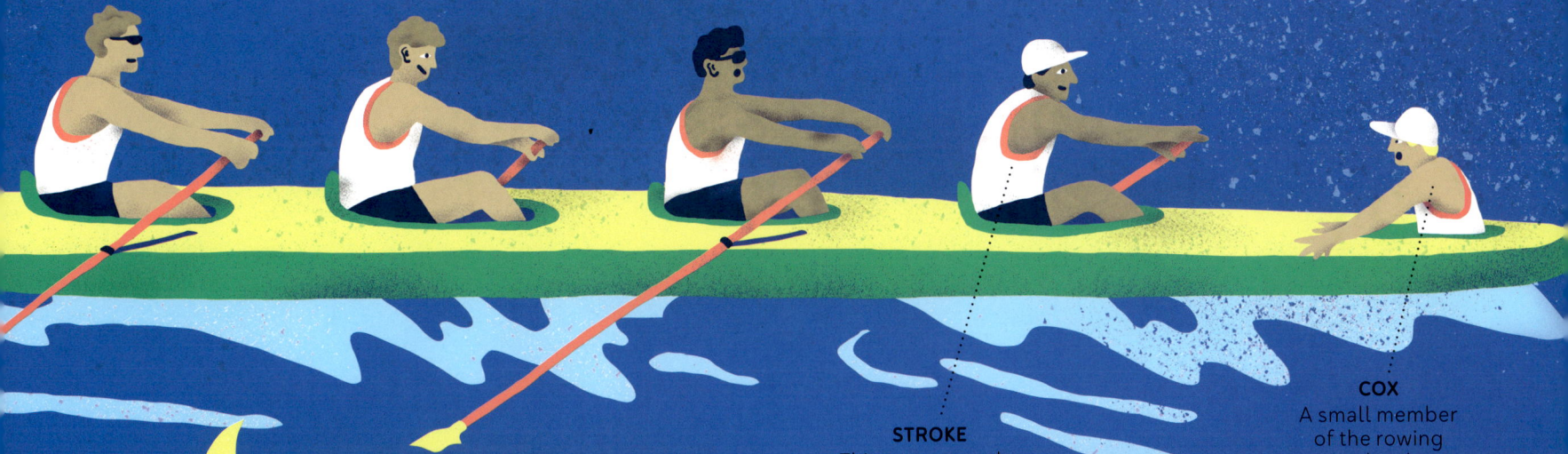

STROKE
This rower sets the timing and rhythm of the oars in the water. They're usually the best rower in the boat too.

COX
A small member of the rowing team who shouts directions at the rest of them.

Sound Like a Pro

"SHELL"
— Another name for a boat.

"ENGINE ROOM"
— The middle rowers in a boat, who provide most of the power.

"BLADES"
— Another name for oars.

"SCULL"
— To row with an oar in each hand.

"SWEEP"
— To row with both hands on one oar.

BEST EVER

USA, Germany and Great Britain have always been the strongest powerhouses in rowing. USA has 89 medals in total, 33 gold.

Great Britain's Sir Steve Redgrave has six Olympic medals, five gold, while Romanian Elisabeta Lipă has eight medals, including five golds too.

REDGRAVE'S MEDAL COUNT: ① X5 ③ X1

LIPĂ'S MEDAL COUNT: ① X5 ② X2 ③ X1

UPSIDES

Rowing is a great sport for building your fitness and making friends by working as a team. You also get to eat loads of food to keep your energy levels up.

DOWNSIDES

Training is hardcore, with early morning starts in all kinds of weather. Rowers are often so exhausted at the end of the race that they collapse.

SAILING

WHAT IS IT?

Sailors must sail their choice of boat around a course, trying to be faster than their opponents, battling the wind and currents.

TWO SAILORS

In most races there are two sailors – one steering and the other working sails.

A TRAPEZE WIRE

Sometimes the crew have to lean right outside the boat to balance the weight, but they stay attached by a trapeze wire connected to the top of the mast.

MAIN SAIL

Boats may have to sail in a zigzag pattern along the course as they use their sails to catch winds in different directions.

BEST EVER

Being an island nation, Great Britain really do 'rule the waves', as the famous song goes. They have 64 medals, 31 of those gold.

Great Britain's Sir Ben Ainslie is one of the most successful sailors at the Olympics with five medals, four gold.

AINSLIE'S MEDAL COUNT: 1 X4   2 X1

Sound Like a Pro

"KNOT" – A measure of speed.

"STARBOARD" – The right-hand side of the boat.

"PORT" – The left-hand side of the boat.

"WINDWARD" – The side closest to the wind.

"SHEET" – A rope used to control a sail.

MARKER BUOY
The course is set out with various markers, and crews will jostle to sail closest to the mark.

A CLOSER LOOK

BASIC TRAINING

Fold several pieces of paper into a fleet of small boats. Colour the sails with flags from countries around the world and then place them in a bath filled with water. Get a handheld fan and point it at the bath to create wind. Then watch all the boats float around for six hours and try to work out which boat has won the race.

SKILLS NEEDED

Sailing is very physically and mentally tough. It's not all sitting on the deck, having a nice picnic and looking at the sky. Sailors can be competing for six hours a day, physically battling with their sails while mentally processing huge amounts of information about wind speed, currents, clouds and tides. Intelligence and good seamanship are crucial, especially when the water beneath you is constantly changing.

The Rules

There are roughly ten races in each of the eight different events, although just to be different the 49er class has 15 races. Boats get points for their finishing positions in each race, so you get one point for coming first, two points for coming second, and so on. Ten boats advance to the medal race, in which points are doubled. The boat with the lowest score wins.

It can be hard for spectators to tell what is going on, especially if they've forgotten their binoculars.

UPSIDES

Catch the right wind in your sail and you'll be flying along, leaving everyone else behind. It takes a lot of effort to do well in so many races, so you really earn your medal.

DOWNSIDES

It's very hard work and you're out at sea for a long time. Sailors tend to be tactically brutal with each other so you might not make friends here.

THE HISTORY BIT

Sailing has been around since cavemen realised that floating on water was better than drowning in it. After that, people continued to use boats for moving things around the world, and for fighting. Then someone decided boats could be fun and sailing joined the Olympics in 1900. It was cancelled in 1904 because there weren't enough boats but rejoined in 1908. It was called yachting until 2000.

INJURIES

Cuts, bruises and hand injuries from rope burn are common. So is banging your head on the boom of the sail. Drowning is rare, as you should have a lifejacket on.

CHANCE OF BECOMING A CHAMPION

| Slim | OK | ↑ | Good | Great |

Sailing is not a cheap sport and you need to live near a large body of water. If you do have access to a boat, then your chances are much improved.

KITESURFING

WHAT IS IT?

Riding a small surfboard that appears to float over the water while being pulled along by a massive kite.

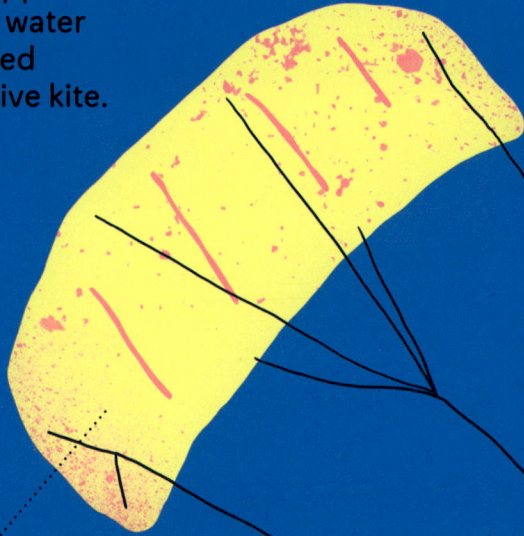

BASIC TRAINING

Get on a skateboard and hold the arms of a really big, puffy jacket, then wait for a massive gust of wind to drag you along. Don't do this on a day with no wind or you'll be standing on the board for ages.

UPSIDES

Kitesurfing takes cool to another level, plus it's really fun. Nobody has ever watched a kitesurfer and said "that looks boring".

DOWNSIDES

You will get hit by a lot of water, especially if you keep falling off. Looking after your equipment can be fiddly, especially if your lines get knotted up.

FOIL KITE

Nothing like those simple kites you might get stuck in a tree on a windy day. This is more like a parachute as it has lots of open sections in it that inflate the foil to help harness the wind. The bright colours help spectators pick out who is winning.

HELMET

This will help if you bang your head.

WETSUIT

You might need one of these if the water is chilly.

BAR AND LINES

The lines stop the foil from flying away and the bar is what you hold on to.

SKILLS NEEDED

Lots of balance and good core strength to pull against the wind and direct your hydrofoil where you want it to go, otherwise you will float off into the distance! However, technique is key over being super strong.

HARNESS

Connects the rider to the bar and lines and can help with balance and steering.

HYDROFOIL

A fast surfboard attached to a fin that lifts the board above the water at certain speeds.

The History Bit

Kitesurfing is a fairly modern sport, but its origins supposedly go way back to 13th-century China, where kite sails were attached to small boats to give them extra speed. Kitesurfing as we know it today was developed over the 1970s and 80s, and the first official competition was held in the late 1990s.

The Rules

Fitting into the sailing category at the Olympics, kitesurfing will involve riders racing each other around a course at high speed, usually around 74 kilometres per hour. Heats will take around ten minutes, leading to a final race where the medals will be awarded.

WINDSURFING

SKILLS NEEDED

More physically demanding than kitesurfing, you need to be strong and athletic to carry out all the manoeuvres and steering.

WHAT IS IT?

Steering a board with one sail attached to it across the water using the power of the wind. All done while standing up.

The Rules

Windsurfers compete in a sailing category called the IQfoil and are awarded points for the position they finish in — the higher you finish the lower the points. At the end of the race series, the top ten with the lowest points have a final race for a medal. You can't smack into your rivals to knock them out of the race, it's not dodgems.

SAIL
A big, old mainsail which is really hard to fit in your car or garage.

LIFE JACKET
Stops you drowning.

WETSUIT
Stops your body freezing in cold water.

HELMET
Protects your brain in case you hit it on some rocks.

HARNESS
The line that attaches the windsurfer to the boom.

BOOM
You need this to hold on to the sail, a bit like handlebars on a bike.

UPSIDES

Great exercise and easy to learn, the kind of sport you can do on a summer holiday. If you get really good, the tricks look spectacular.

DOWNSIDES

Anyone have room for a nine-metre sail in their house? Arguments with kitesurfers over which sport is better get boring after a while.

FOOTSTRAPS
Help to keep your feet in place while you carry out manoeuvres.

BOARD
Windsurfers can choose between a hydrofoil or regular fin, which is a board with an erm . . . fin sticking into the water underneath that helps your stability and stops the board drifting off in the wrong direction.

BEST EVER

There's a good spread of medals but the Dutch top the men's event with four golds, while France and China have two golds each in the women's category.

ATHLETICS
Track Events

WHAT IS IT?

Athletes run around a big, oval track as fast as possible, and for various distances. To make it slightly trickier, some athletes have to jump over things, while others have to pass a baton.

SINGLET
To keep cool, most distance runners wear loose-fitting, lightweight sleeveless vests.

LIGHTWEIGHT SHORT SHORTS
Made from a breathable fabric.

BASIC TRAINING

Running is one of the easiest sports to train for — you have the whole world to jog around.

Sound Like a Pro

"PACEMAKER"
— A runner who deliberately sets a fast pace. They drop out before the finish and let other athletes win.

"DEAD HEAT"
— When it's impossible to tell who has won a race and it's called a tie.

"ANCHOR LEG"
— The last runner in the relay team, usually the fastest.

"FALSE START"
— Moving before the starting gun has been fired.

INJURIES

Legs, hips, knees, groin, ankles and feet take the most punishment, so make sure you warm up and cool down properly.

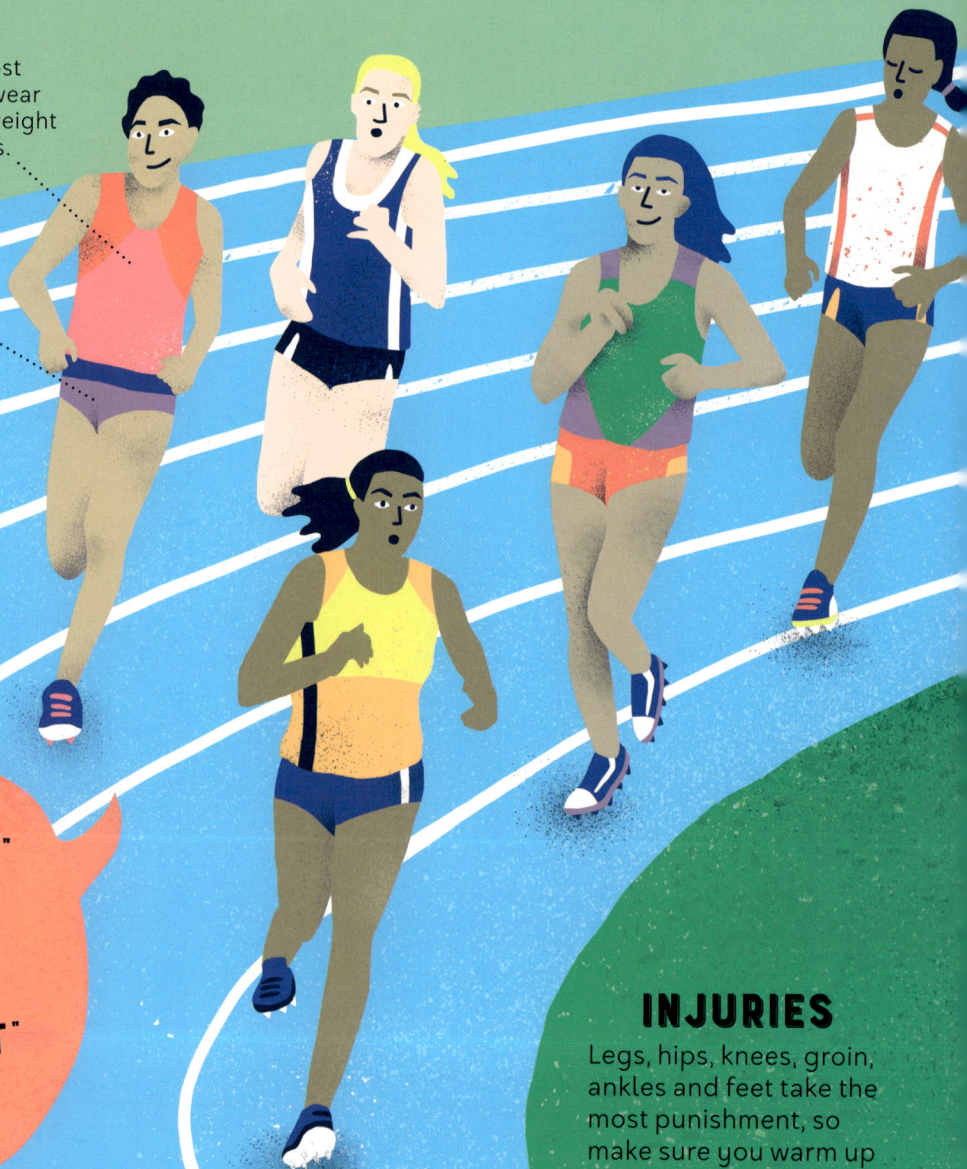

The History Bit

Cavemen probably invented running while being chased by a sabre-toothed tiger. However, most of the time the cavemen weren't quick enough and ended up as dinner. Because running is so simple, it's no surprise that it was one of the sports in the first modern Olympics in 1896. Women's events were added in 1928, and athletics were in the first Paralympics in 1960.

EPIC FAIL

800-metre runner Wim Esajas, from Suriname, apparently overslept and missed his one and only heat at the 1960 Olympics. However, it was later discovered he was given the wrong starting time by officials.

HIGH HURDLES

These are L-shaped and designed to fall forwards if runners clip them as they jump, which avoids getting their legs in a nasty tangle.

POWERFUL LUNGS

Distance runners need an incredible amount of stamina to keep up a fast and steady pace for a long time.

A CLOSER LOOK

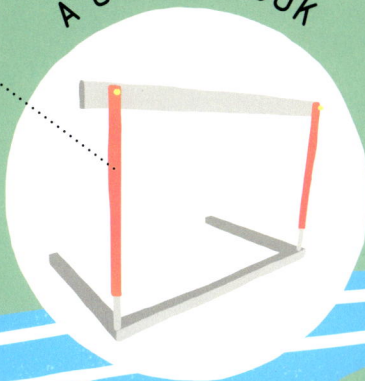

SPIKED RUNNING SHOES

Athletes wear special shoes to absorb the impact of each step, with spikes for added grip.

UPSIDES

Telling everyone you are the fastest person on the planet is an impressive bit of bragging and successful track athletes are some of the most famous people in the world.

DOWNSIDES

Training is hard and long-distance runners spend a long time away from home. Sprinters can get injured very easily and coming fourth in a race must be one of the worst feelings ever.

BEST EVER

USA's Carl Lewis has nine golds and one silver, in 100 metres, 200 metres, 4 x 100 metres relay and the long jump. Jamaica's Usain Bolt has eight golds in 100 metres, 200 metres and 4 x 100 metres relay. Maybe he should have done the long jump too! Bolt is currently the world-record holder in 100 metres and 200 metres. So, he's the fastest person on the planet!

USA's Allyson Felix has 11 medals, seven gold.

Swiss wheelchair athlete Franz Nietlispach has won 14 gold, six silver and two bronze medals at the Paralympics.

NIETLISPACH'S MEDAL COUNT: 1 X14   2 X6   3 X2

THE EVENTS

SPRINTING

• 100 metres • 200 metres • 400 metres
• 4 x 100 metres relay • 4 x 400 metres relay

There are the same distances at the Paralympics but with 15 different classifications depending on impairment. The 100 metres is the biggest event at every Olympics, even though it's over in around ten seconds. Sprinters have to have explosive power to sprint very quickly for a very short period of time – 45 seconds for 400 metres, which is one whole lap of the track.

HURDLES

• 110 metres (for men) • 100 metres (for women)
• 400 metres (men and women)

Runners must sprint and clear ten hurdles as fast as possible before the finish line. Hurdles are usually waist height, so it takes skill to get over them without breaking your stride or falling flat on your face.

MIDDLE DISTANCE

• 800 metres (two laps around the track) • 1,500 metres (three and three-quarter laps) • 3,000-metre steeplechase (with hurdles and a water pit to jump)

These are more tactical races, with a mixture of jogging and sprinting. Runners bunch up together and are constantly checking over their shoulders to see where their rivals are before they get ready to sprint the last lap.

LONG DISTANCE

• 5,000 metres (12 and a half laps) • 10,000 metres (25 laps) • marathon (26.2 miles around a city)

These events are true tests of stamina, endurance, mental toughness and another tactical battle with your rivals. Your whole body will be saying, "This isn't fun any more. Can we stop now for a sit down?". Long-distance runners are very different from their muscular sprinting teammates – they're usually wiry with hardly any body fat.

RACE WALKING

• 20 kilometres • 50 kilometres (for men only)

Walking is the sport where everyone looks like they are trying to get to the toilet as quickly as possible. Athletes must make sure one foot appears to be on the ground at all times. Failure to do this is called a 'loss of contact'. Three of these and you get a red card and are out. Imagine walking 49 kilometres and getting a red card on your final lap!

ATHLETICS
Field Events

WHAT IS IT?

The throwing and jumping side of athletics, done in the middle of the oval track while everyone is really watching the runners.

The Rules

All throwers and jumpers get several attempts to record their best distances or heights to beat their rivals. It's important to yell at the top of your lungs after your throw. This makes your hammer, javelin, discus or shot very scared and it will travel a little bit further away from you.

HIGH JUMP

FOSBURY FLOP
This jumping technique is named after Dick Fosbury, a 1968 high-jump champion.

ODD SHOES
To give high jumpers an extra spring in their step, some wear one shoe with tiny spikes on the sole.

HIGH BAR
The bar gets higher and higher as the competition goes on.

A SINGLET AND SHORTS
Keeping it simple.

SOFT LANDING
The mat is usually at least one metre thick to cushion the landing.

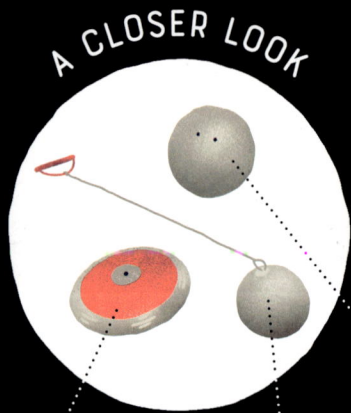

A CLOSER LOOK

DISCUS
A small, heavy, plate-sized disc.

HAMMER
A metal ball attached to a wire with a grip handle on the end.

SHOT
A shot is about the same weight as a bowling ball.

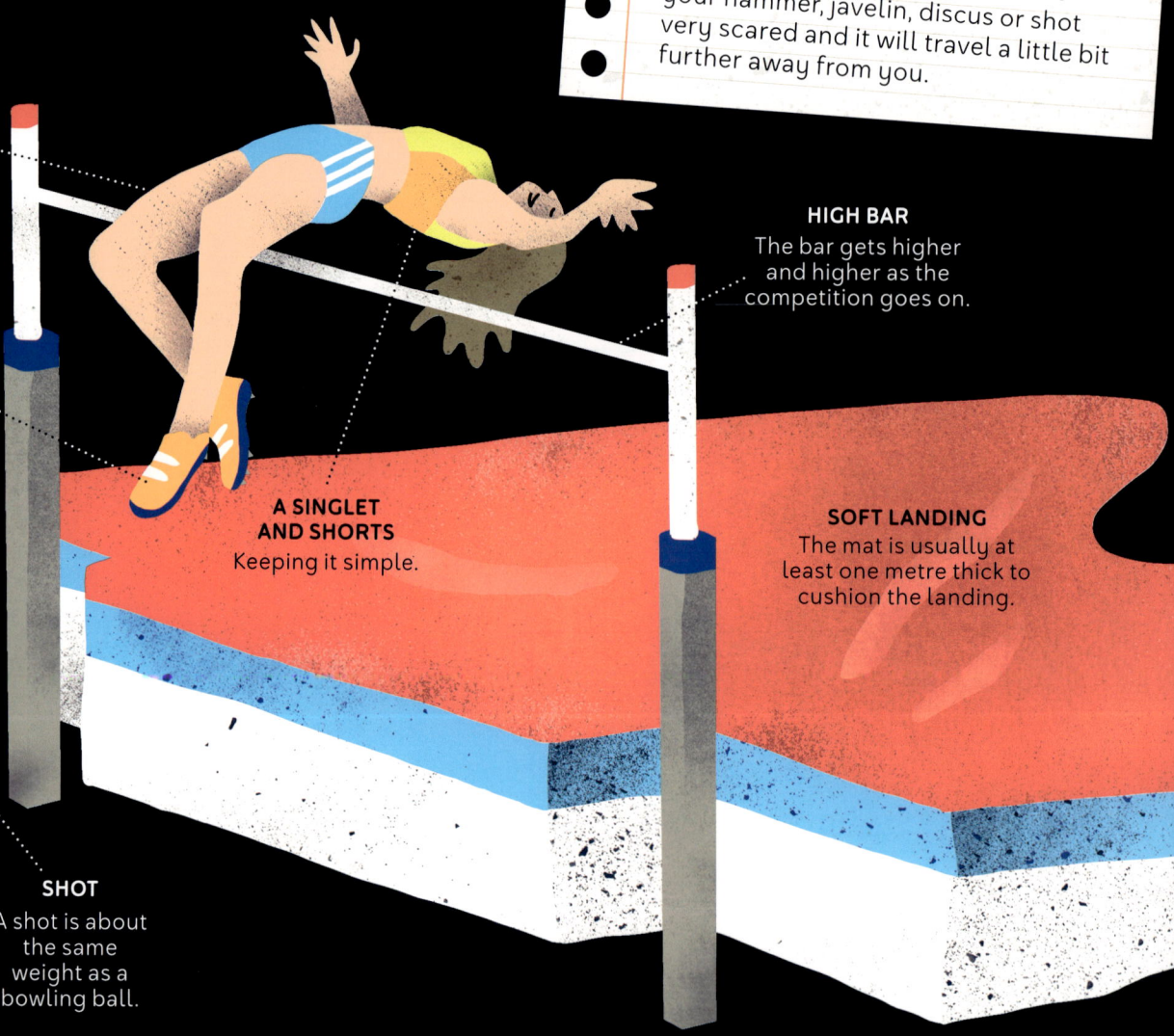

THE EVENTS

TRIPLE JUMP

For athletes who want to make the long jump more fun — add a hop and a skip before jumping into the big sandpit.

LONG JUMP

Sprint down the runway until you reach a white board, then leap forward as far as you can, landing in a sandpit so you don't hurt your bottom. If you step over the board, your jump doesn't count.

HIGH JUMP

Jumpers try to jump over a bar without knocking it down. They attempt this by doing a 'Fosbury flop' where they leap head first then arch their back over the bar. All jumpers must take off on one foot. They land on a big, chunky mat, otherwise it would really hurt.

POLE VAULT

Pole vaulters sprint down a runway carrying a long pole. When they get to the end, they plant the pole into a box and swing their way up into the air and, hopefully, over a very high bar.

Challenging each other to throw things further or jump higher than anyone else has been around for thousands of years. Javelin, discus and long jump were included in the ancient Olympic games. Discus and long jump were in the first modern Olympics in 1896, with javelin added in 1908.

The 1896 games also included triple jump, which was probably based on playground hopscotch; high jump, which started in Scotland in the 1800s; pole vault, which began as a way for people to quickly get over rivers and marshes; and shot put, which came from soldiers chucking cannonballs around in the Middle Ages. The hammer throw also started in the Middle Ages, when people hurled the blacksmith's hammer while he wasn't looking, and joined the Olympics in 1900.

SKILLS NEEDED

Throwers need strength, power and timing. Jumpers need feet made of springs.

SHOT PUT

CHALK ON THEIR HANDS
Throwers use chalk to keep whatever they're throwing from slipping.

TIGHT LEGGINGS
As it can get a bit chilly waiting around for your next go.

THROWING CIRCLE
This has a non-slippery surface so throwers don't slip as they're spinning.

BASIC TRAINING

It's all about the shouting. First thing in the morning, leap out of bed, stamp both feet on the ground and roar like a polar bear with a headache. In the afternoon, when you get home from school, burst through the front door and bellow like a camel with a sore foot. Do this twice. Then, in the evening, walk round the house clapping until the rest of your family start to join in with the rhythm, then go and jump over the sofa.

Sound Like a Pro

"CAGE"
— A high fence around the throwing circle in discus and hammer throw. This stops the crowd getting hit in the face if a throw goes wrong.

"IMPACT AREA"
— Where the javelin, shot, discus and hammer are supposed to land after being thrown. Judges stand here and try not to get hit.

"FLIGHT PHASE"
— The time a jumper is in the air.

"TAKE-OFF BOARD"
— Where a triple or long jumper takes off from.

JAVELIN THROW

Charge down the runway carrying your long spear level with your head. Chuck it into the air as high and far as you can. Make sure you don't step over the fault line at the end of the runway or your throw won't count.

SHOT PUT

Start with a metal ball tucked under your chin and near your neck, then hurl it above shoulder height as far as you can without stepping out of the throwing circle.

DISCUS THROW

Put your hand over the top of your discus, then spin around the throwing circle until you reach top speed and throw. Luckily, the discus doesn't smash like a plate when it hits the ground.

HAMMER THROW

Spin round and round and round and round, then let go, zinging your hammer high into the air as far as it will possibly go. At the Paralympics, athletes throw a wooden club instead.

Athletics
DECATHLON and HEPTATHLON

WHAT IS IT?
A multisport track and field event for the superhuman desperate to prove they are the 'World's Greatest Athlete'.

THE EVENTS
- SPRINTING (m/w)
- LONG JUMP (m/w)
- SHOT PUT (m/w)
- HIGH JUMP (m/w)
- MIDDLE DISTANCE (m/w)
- HURDLES (m/w)
- DISCUS THROW (m)
- POLE VAULT (m)
- JAVELIN THROW (m/w)
- 1,500 METRES (m)

m = men   w = women

A CLOSER LOOK

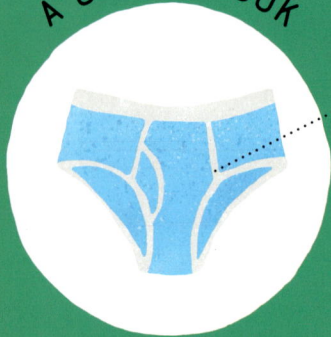

LUCKY PANTS
Athletes probably change their clothes between events, but they might have a pair of lucky pants that they have to keep on at all times.

1 SPRINTING (100/200 METRES)
Imagine being chased by an angry cheetah.

2 LONG JUMP
You'll get lots of sand up your shorts.

3 SHOT PUT
Chucking a heavy metal ball, which leaves a massive dent in the field.

4 HIGH JUMP
This is jumping over a really high bar – basically the opposite of limbo.

5 MIDDLE DISTANCE (400/800 METRES)
Imagine being chased by an angry bear.

INJURIES
There are way more events, so way more chance of injuries.

The Rules

Decathlon is for men and is ten events across two days – 100 metres, long jump, shot put, high jump, 400 metres, 110-metres hurdles, discus throw, pole vault, javelin throw and 1,500 metres.

Heptathlon is for women and is seven events across two days – 100-metres hurdles, high jump, shot put, 200 metres, long jump, javelin throw and 800 metres.

Athletes score points for how well they perform in each event and the one with the most points at the end is the winner. They also have to fit in going for a wee, having a snack and getting extra advice from their coach in the short breaks between events.

CHANCE OF BECOMING A CHAMPION

| Slim ↑ | OK | Good | Great |

You have to be a spectacular athlete to even think about doing the decathlon or heptathlon. Most competitors are so good they would have a chance of winning a medal even if they entered one of the single events!

The History Bit

The decathlon and heptathlon can be traced back to the ancient Olympics, when organisers got so fed up with athletes bragging about how good they were that they invented a five-part event called pentathlon, with sprint, javelin, discus, long jump and wrestling.

The 1904 Olympics featured an all-round event, which became the decathlon in 1912. They quickly dropped the wrestling though as nobody liked getting beaten up. Women started pentathlon in 1964, which became heptathlon in 1984.

BASIC TRAINING

There is no time for basic training. You must do real training all the time — as soon as you wake up until it gets dark, and even when you're in bed and in your dreams. If you get up for a wee in the night, also do ten press-ups.

Sound Like a Pro

"OWWW, THIS REALLY HURTS"

"I WANT MY MUMMY"

"WHAT DO YOU MEAN THERE ARE STILL SEVEN EVENTS LEFT?!"

(This is probably what you'd be saying to yourself after one day of competing!)

UPSIDES

If you win Olympic gold, you are officially the 'World's Greatest Athlete'.

DOWNSIDES

It is mentally and physically exhausting. Some people call it the toughest sport on earth.

6 HURDLES
Trying to run fast when someone's put little fences in the way.

7 DISCUS THROW
Throwing a chunky plate as far as possible.

8 POLE VAULT
This is basically flying using a really long stick.

SKILLS NEEDED

Everything! Strength, speed, power, great stamina, a spring in your heels . . . the list goes on. Usually, athletes specialise in a handful of events that will give them maximum points, so they don't have to do that well in others. For example, a good decathlete might do really well in eight events, which should give them enough points to not do so well in the other two events.

9 JAVELIN THROW
This would be more fun if it was called spear hurling.

10 1,500 METRES
Imagine being chased by an angry duck.

65

GYMNASTICS

Rings

ARTISTIC

WHAT IS IT?

Very bendy athletes compete in a series of different events, with amazing acrobatic routines and feats of strength.

THE APPARATUS

- BALANCE BEAM (w)
- FLOOR (m/w)
- HORIZONTAL BAR (m)
- PARALLEL BARS (m)
- POMMEL HORSE (m)
- RINGS (m)
- UNEVEN BARS (w)
- VAULT (m/w)

m = men   w = women

SKILLS NEEDED

You need to be flexible and strong, with a sense of style and, most importantly, courage. Gymnasts are usually small, compact and powerful. You don't get many over 6 feet tall.

BASIC TRAINING

Start with a simple handstand, then walk around doing a handstand, then do a one-handed press-up in a handstand. Now walk to the shops doing a handstand and do a double backwards somersault into the shop. See? Gymnastics is simple!

INJURIES

Severe injuries are rare, but your ankles, wrists, knees, feet, back and hands will get a tough going over — especially with bad landings.

LEOTARDS
Female gymnasts call it a leotard; males prefer to call them singlets or competition shirts. They are tight-fitting so the judges can always see the shape of the gymnast's moves.

CHUNKY WRIST BANDS AND HAND SUPPORTS
To protect themselves from injuries.

Sound Like a Pro

"GIANT"
— A full rotation of the bar in a handstand position.

"RIP"
— A blister, usually on the hand or wrist.

"MOUNT/DISMOUNT"
— To get on or off the apparatus.

"STICK"
— To make a perfect landing.

"SALTO"
— A fancy name for a flip or somersault.

BEST EVER

The Soviet Union (USSR) was home to the best artistic gymnasts, with 182 medals, 72 gold. USA is next with 117, then Japan with 103.

Russia's Larisa Latynina holds the record for most Olympic gymnastic medals, with 18, nine of those gold. She is the most successful female Olympian in any sport, and second only to American swimmer Michael Phelps in the all-time most Olympic medals list.

LATYNINA'S MEDAL COUNT: ① X9 ② X5 ③ X4

CHANCE OF BECOMING A CHAMPION

Slim — OK — Good — Great

You need to be super bendy and strong to even climb on most of the apparatus. Gymnasts are usually selected at a very young age.

The History Bit

Gymnastics can be traced back to ancient Greece, where soldiers used gymnastic moves to get ready for war. They did all this with no clothes on, only stopping to get dressed when it was time to battle. In the 1700s, different types of apparatus were invented, and were first used by the military, schools and sports clubs.

Artistic gymnastics became one of the first sports to appear at the modern games in 1896, with a women's team event joining in 1928. Further women's events arrived a bit later in 1952.

UPSIDES

It's easy to impress someone if you can do a flying double somersault.

DOWNSIDES

Training is long and hard. You need to be incredibly committed to learn skills on all the different apparatus.

BALANCE BEAM (WOMEN)

Gymnasts perform a routine of jumps, leaps and flips on a thin wooden beam no wider than their feet.

FLOOR (MEN AND WOMEN)

A routine on a big mat, usually with lots of flying somersaults.

HORIZONTAL BAR (MEN)

One bar which gymnasts swing, flip and twist themselves around, sometimes flying into the air hoping to catch the bar on the way down.

PARALLEL BARS (MEN)

Gymnasts swing, balance and lift themselves using two high bars that are next to each other. Call them P-bars to sound cool.

POMMEL HORSE (MEN)

A headless, tailless horse, with two handles (pommels) in the middle. Gymnasts swing their legs around the horse and support the rest of their body with their hands.

RINGS (MEN)

Gymnasts perform muscle-crunching moves while clinging on to two high rings hanging from a metal frame. Super-strength is needed — it's the gymnastic version of weightlifting.

UNEVEN BARS (WOMEN)

Two bars at different heights which gymnasts swing between and perform tricks from.

VAULT (MEN AND WOMEN)

Gymnasts sprint down a runway, leap off a springboard and throw themselves towards the vault to perform a mid-air pirouette or something equally amazing. Then they have to land perfectly on the other side.

A CLOSER LOOK

CHALK
To help with grip and to stop the gymnast from getting sweaty hands.

Pommel Horse

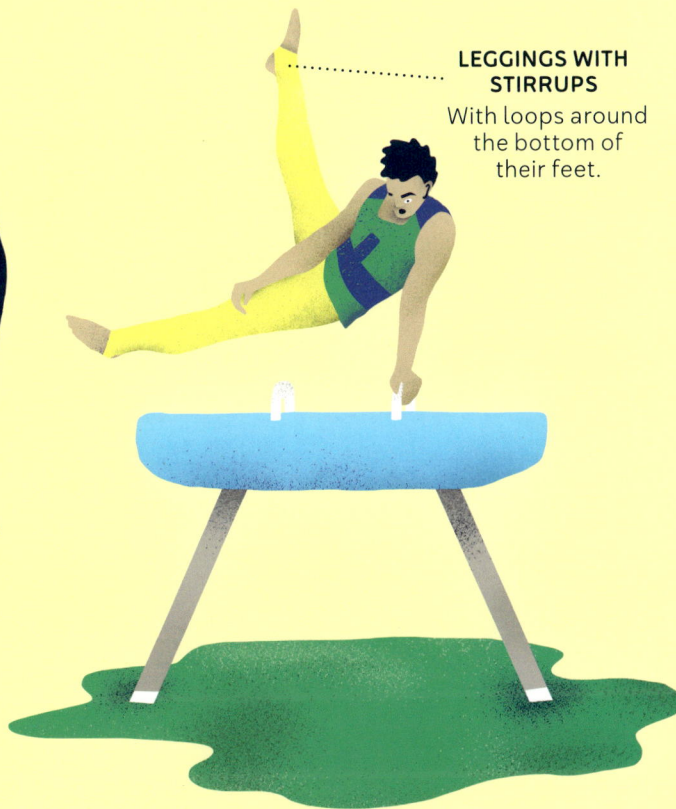

LEGGINGS WITH STIRRUPS
With loops around the bottom of their feet.

BARE FEET, SOCKS OR SOFT SHOES
This depends on the event.

SPARKLE
Female athletes' make-up, hair and leotards get the full treatment. This hasn't spread to the men's event yet.

Balance Beam

67

GYMNASTICS
Trampoline

WHAT IS IT?

The closest an athlete will get to flying, with a few bouncy acrobatic tricks thrown in.

LEOTARDS
Trampolinists wear the same as other gymnasts. Some men may wear a vest and tight-fitting trousers.

The Rules

Athletes get ten bounces to perform a series of acrobatic tricks, somersaults, twists and other crazy moves. Judges award points for difficulty, execution and flight time (there are actually points for flying!). You lose points for failing to do a trick, falling or landing badly. Whoever has the most points at the end is the winner.

Sound Like a Pro

"BED"
— This is the part of the trampoline you jump on.

"KILLER"
— A double back somersault with four twists.

"FLIFFUS"
— A double somersault with at least a half twist.

"SPOTTER"
— The person who tries to catch you if you fall.

BASIC TRAINING

Just jump up and down on your parents' bed. When they come in to tell you off, leap over their heads with a flying somersault and run away.

The History Bit

Today's trampoline wasn't invented until 1935, and it was first used to train astronauts! The Olympics didn't discover that trampolining could be fun until 2000.

A BIG, RECTANGULAR TRAMPOLINE
It's usually about 5 metres long by 3 metres wide, so not like the round ones you put in your garden.

RED CROSS
This marks the centre of the jumping zone.

A LOAD OF BIG PADS AND MATS
In case you fall off.

INJURIES
All over — arms, legs, neck and face. Landing badly on any of these body parts is going to leave a big bruise.

SKILLS NEEDED
You need to be able to twist your body into the shape of a pretzel. It also helps if you have a head for heights, as you could go as high as ten metres off the ground — that's about three elephants standing on top of one another!

UPSIDES
Unless you are planning on growing wings, this is your best chance to fly.

DOWNSIDES
It can get very messy if you get your trick or bounce wrong and you end up flying through the air out of control.

RHYTHMIC

WHAT IS IT?

Female gymnasts perform ballet moves, leaps, tumbles, pirouettes and other fancy gymnastic tricks while using bits of kit you'd find in the school sports cupboard.

THE APPARATUS
- RIBBON
- HOOP
- CLUBS
- BALL

The Rules

For the individual event, gymnasts perform once with each bit of apparatus. In the team event, five gymnasts perform twice using different bits of apparatus at the same time. Judges award points for things like dancing, how gymnasts use the apparatus and how good it all looks. The highest score wins.

BASIC TRAINING

Start with the ribbon as it looks like the easiest, but probably isn't. Flick it repeatedly at your dad while he's trying to watch television. When he chases you out of the room, leave a club, a ball and a hoop by the door so he trips over them.

LONG RIBBON ATTACHED TO A SHORT STICK

The gymnast flicks, circles, spirals and snakes the ribbon and, to make it really hard, throws it into the air.

LEOTARD COVERED IN TWINKLY BITS

It's all about sparkle, glitz and glamour.

Sound Like a Pro

"ARABESQUE" — Standing on one leg with the other in the air at a 45-degree angle.

"AERIAL CARTWHEEL" — A cartwheel, but in mid-air.

"SPLIT LEAP" — The splits, but in mid-air.

SLIPPERS
Special half-shoes that only cover the front of the foot.

A CLOSER LOOK

LARGE PLASTIC OR WOODEN HOOP
For swinging, throwing, catching and leaping through.

RUBBER BALL
About the size of your head. It's thrown, caught, bounced and rolled.

SOFT-ISH CLUBS, A BIT LIKE BOWLING PINS
For spinning, throwing and catching. Sadly, they are not set on fire. You lose points for drops.

The History Bit

In the olden days, emperors, kings and evil warlords watched acrobats perform and usually killed the ones they didn't like. This went on for hundreds of years, until the 1800s when it turned into a version of rhythmic gymnastics and nobody got killed. The Russians made it into a sport in the 1940s, because they were really good at it, and it became properly competitive in the 1960s. Rhythmic gymnastics joined the Olympics in 1984 and the team part was added in 1996.

SKILLS NEEDED

You need to be flexible, agile, coordinated and have a sense of style and grace. This probably isn't for you if you're clumsy.

UPSIDES

It's very popular with the crowds because it's exciting to watch the amazing routines.

DOWNSIDES

A lot of long training sessions that make your body feel like it might snap in half.

CHANCE OF BECOMING A CHAMPION

Slim	OK	Good	Great

If you've been dancing since you could walk, then you might have a chance.

BREAKING

WHAT IS IT?

B-Boys and B-Girls battle against each other, pulling off a series of acrobatic street dance moves while a DJ plays fast-tempo beats.

BASIC TRAINING

Put on a fast song and dance in front of the mirror — if you don't look like your granny at a wedding, you can try out some basic breaking moves.

The Rules

One event for B-Boys (men) and one for B-Girls (women). Sixteen athletes in each event go head-to-head in battles. Despite the word 'battles', breaking, like skateboarding, is a friendly, community-based sport. Breakers encourage their rivals when they do an impressive move and the having-fun element is often more important than the medal.

Sound Like a Pro

"THROW DOWN"
When a B-Boy or B-Girl takes to the floor to start their routine.

"BITING"
When another breaker accuses you of copying or pinching their moves. You don't want this.

"FRESH"
Something good.

"CRASHING"
Failing an attempted move.

"ROASTED/ SMOKED"
Losing a battle badly.

"WHACK"
Something bad.

TOP MOVES

TOPROCK

A series of steps to get your set going.

DOWNROCK

Includes basic breaking moves like the 3-step and 6-step, where you use your arms to manoeuvre your body around the floor while circling your legs in the air.

BRIDGE

A move where you raise your chest upwards and bend both arms and legs backwards to the floor to hold you up.

SKILLS NEEDED

Let's start with strength, stamina, flexibility and plenty of energy. Patience to practise all the moves and to fail lots of time. Bravery, creativity and self-expression help you stand out from the other competitors. A dull routine won't win.

INJURIES

Because of the complex and repetitive nature of many moves, breaking and injuries sadly go hand in hand. Most of your body will get a good thwacking eventually.

The History Bit

Breaking started in the early 1970s on street corners in New York, USA, using elements of other dance and sport styles such as capoeira, disco, lindy hop, gymnastics and martial arts. It quickly took off around the world — in the 1980s, pop stars started using styles of breaking in their videos and everyone soon tried to give it a go. For a laugh, ask one of your parents to show you some moves.

CHANCE OF BECOMING A CHAMPION

Slim	OK	Good	Great

Breaking is a sport anyone can have a go at and doesn't require lots of expensive gear. Your body is your equipment. But you better start practising now, as breaking takes a long time to master.

UPSIDES

Breaking is probably the coolest sport at the Olympics (shh, don't tell the skateboarders or BMXers). It's high energy, super-friendly and amazing to watch.

DOWNSIDES

Get it wrong and breaking will hurt. Slamming your body on to a hard floor to win the judges' approval takes lots of guts.

WINDMILL

A power move where you twirl your legs in the air while rolling your body around the floor.

FREEZE

A stylish pose, usually featuring the breaker holding themselves up with one hand. Moving through different freezes is called 'stacking'.

HEADSPIN

A power move where you spin on your head without any support. Power moves rely on acrobatics and speed more than other moves.

Sport Climbing

WHAT IS IT?

Being able to be higher up up than everyone else is one of the great things about being a human. Astronaut, mountaineer, stilt walker and very tall person are all great jobs, but you can get a shiny gold medal if you become an Olympic sport climber.

The Rules

Olympic sport climbing is actually three events in one:
1) Speed climbing: two climbers race against each other up a 15-metre wall.
2) Bouldering: each climber scales a course on a four-metre wall in a fixed time.
3) Lead climbing: a race to climb the highest in a fixed time.
The best person at all three events will win gold.

BASIC TRAINING

It all starts with a bunk bed. Don't use the ladder – practise climbing to the top bunk and note down your fastest time. If you don't have a bunk bed, find a tree. But be very careful – trees don't come with mattresses to fall on if you make a mistake.

SAFETY ROPE
Usually made of nylon, it needs to be strong and flexible.

A CLOSER LOOK

BEST EVER

Spain's Alberto Ginés López won the first men's combined medal at the 2021 Olympics, while Slovenia's Janja Garnbret scooped the women's medal – she had already won World and European titles. As this is a fairly new Olympic sport, keep an eye out for any countries who have entered a squirrel as a competitor. They will probably win gold, but they might keep stopping to hide their nuts.

NEAR-VERTICAL WALL
As it's hard to move a mountain and put it into an arena, climbers have to use a very high wall instead.

BRIGHTLY COLOURED HAND, FINGER AND FOOT HOLDS
These help you climb up the walls and plan your route in advance.

BARE HANDS ONLY
You aren't allowed to wear gloves and you need to make sure you've trimmed your fingernails.

CHALK
To keep your hands dry and help with grip.

EXTREMELY TIGHT, SOFT SHOES
These help climbers' feet grip the wall.

SKILLS NEEDED

You need to be strong, agile, flexible, have fingertips made of iron as well as a powerful grip. You also need a strategic brain to plan your route carefully. It's no good being fast if you find yourself climbing on to the roof of the supermarket by mistake.

Sound Like a Pro

"GUMBY" – An inexperienced climber.

"BETA" – Information on how to complete a climbing route.

"FLATLANDER" – A non-climber.

"CRUX" – The hardest part of a climb.

"PEEL" – To fall.

"FLASH" – To complete a route on the first attempt.

"BIDOIGT" bee-dwah – A climbing hold big enough for just two fingers (French for 'two fingers').

"CUT-LOOSE" – When a climber is hanging by just their hands.

CHALK BAG
This is for chalk, not tasty snacks on the way up.

UPSIDES

Climbing to the very top faster than anyone else is a huge thrill and a great confidence boost. Once you've climbed to the top of a high wall or mountain, you feel like you can do anything.

DOWNSIDES

It can be very painful. You'll sometimes have to hold your whole body weight with just two fingers.

INJURIES

Sore fingers and scraped knees are common, but more serious injuries are usually in the shoulders because they do most of the work. The safety ropes prevent most of the nasty injuries.

CHANCE OF BECOMING A CHAMPION

Slim	OK	Good	Great

Most top climbers specialise in just one of the events, so if you can master all three, you've got a great chance.

The History Bit

Cavemen first started climbing to avoid being eaten by sabre-toothed tigers thousands of years ago, but the sport made its first appearance at the Olympics in 2021. Sadly, the sabre-tooth was replaced by a stopwatch.

TRIATHLON

WHAT IS IT?

Three long-distance sports in one — swimming, cycling and running — with no breaks.

The Rules

Olympic triathlon starts with a swim of 1,500 metres, usually in a lake, river or sea, then a 40-kilometre cycle and a 10-kilometre run. Everyone goes at the same time and the first person to cross the finish line wins.

WETSUIT
Straight after the swim, wriggle out of your wetsuit and throw your goggles off.

1

SWIMMING CAP
So people can see your head while you're in the water.

SHORTS AND VEST IN ONE
Your tri-suit, which you wear underneath your wetsuit, can dry as you cycle.

HELMET AND SUNGLASSES
Put these on as you try to clip your feet into bike pedals and cycle off.

2

Sound Like a Pro

"BONK"
— To lose all of your energy.

"BOPER"
— Someone who is at the back of the pack.

"FRED"
— Someone who has all the gear but hardly ever uses it.

"CD"
— Cool down.

CHANCE OF BECOMING A CHAMPION

Slim   OK   Good   Great

Triathlon is growing in popularity around the world and there are also more places up for grabs at the Olympics, with a new mixed relay event, where teams of two men and two women do a 300-metre swim, an 8-kilometre cycle and a 2-kilometre run.

3

The History Bit

Bored with running, some bright spark in the USA decided to throw some more sports into their daily workout and then put together the first modern triathlon in California in the mid-1970s. It became incredibly popular and joined the Olympics in 2000 and the Paralympics in 2016.

SOCKS
It will slow you down to put these on, but they stop blisters.

LOCK LACES
Elastic shoelaces that you don't have to tie up, to save time.

UPSIDES

People are impressed if you say you've done a triathlon, because they are very tough.

DOWNSIDES

Triathlon is THE 'getting changed into different clothes and swapping equipment' sport. Unfortunately, you must do it all mid-race. If it takes you a long time to get dressed, this isn't the sport for you.

MODERN PENTATHLON

WHAT IS IT?

Five different sports — fencing, swimming, riding, shooting and running — packed into one day. A true test of all-round sporting ability.

BEST EVER

Hungary and Sweden top the medal charts, with nine golds each. Hungarian András Balczó has three golds and two silvers.

THE EVENTS
- FENCING
- SWIMMING
- RIDING
- SHOOTING
- RUNNING

RUNNING GEAR
Make sure you give your trainers a good spray beforehand — you don't want them to stink.

FENCING GEAR
It's time to sharpen up your épée again (even though they're blunt).

SKILLS NEEDED
Everything! Apart from mountain-climbing and cooking skills.

SHOOTING GEAR
Sadly, it's shooting a laser pistol at targets, not space aliens.

SWIMMING GEAR
You won't win if you do the breaststroke.

5 1 4 3 2

RIDING GEAR
A random horse is given to you just 20 minutes before you begin show jumping! So you're in big trouble if it's in a bad mood.

INJURIES
All the injuries from the other sports piled on top of each other.

UPSIDES
You do all these sports in one day. It never gets boring.

DOWNSIDES
You do all these sports in one day. It's incredibly exhausting.

CHANCE OF BECOMING A CHAMPION

Slim	OK	Good	Great

Look in your wardrobe. Do you own an épée, laser pistol, show-jumping horse or swimming pool?

The History Bit

The founder of the modern Olympics, Pierre de Coubertin, claimed he thought of this event, basing it on a French soldier who was delivering a message. The poor chap ended up doing all of these things in one day! The men's event started in 1912 and the women's in 2000.

WEIGHTLIFTING

WHAT IS IT?

Athletes lift a series of different heavy weights attached to a bar, and then stand as still as possible for a few seconds.

SKILLS NEEDED

Explosive power and strength. If you struggle to lift a heavy suitcase, this isn't for you. You can be any shape and size to be a top weightlifter. They are put in different categories depending on how heavy they are, anything from bantamweight to super heavyweight.

The Rules

Olympic weightlifting fits into two disciplines. First the 'clean and jerk', which sounds like washing-up while breakdancing, but isn't, and the 'snatch', which sadly isn't about pinching sweets.

In the snatch, weights are lifted in one motion. In clean and jerk, it's two movements – up to the shoulders (the clean), then above the head (the jerk). You have to hold the weight in position above your head with your arms and legs in a straight lock until a buzzer tells you it's time to stop.

Weightlifters have three goes to lift each weight, and if they're successful, the weight is increased.

FINGER AND KNEE TAPE
Weightlifters cover their fingers, thumbs, wrists and knees in tape to help prevent injuries.

CHALK
Lifters throw chalk all over their hands to stop the weight slipping.

SINGLET
Sometimes worn with a T-shirt underneath.

MASSIVE BELT
This supports and stabilises the lifter's spine.

A CLOSER LOOK

WEIGHT DISCS
Sometimes called bumper plates, they are covered in rubber, so they can be dropped from a height without smashing through the floor.

BARBELL
The bumper plates attach to a grippy iron bar.

BASIC TRAINING

Cover yourself in chalk, then get a stick and hang an increasing number of heavy things on the ends. Lift the stick above your head and let out a blood-curdling scream to make it clear that what you're doing is incredibly tough. Make sure you don't lift the heaviest thing straight away or you'll hurt yourself.

FINAL PUSH
The final position of the lift, with straight legs and weight above the head.

COLOUR-CODED WEIGHTS
Different weights are different colours – simple!

GURNING
Weightlifters pull all kinds of unusual faces when lifting. Sometimes it looks like their heads are about to pop off their shoulders.

SHOES WITH A RAISED HEEL
They help the weightlifter squat deeper to generate more power.

KNEES ON DISPLAY
Judges need to be able to see knees and elbows at all times.

INJURIES
Your knees, wrists and shoulders take a battering, although nasty injuries are rare unless you get your technique all wrong.

Sound Like a Pro
"HANG"
– The starting position when you lift the weight off the floor, and usually the moment you realise you've made a big mistake.

"COLLARS"
– The things at the end of the barbell that stop the weights sliding off.

"KNURLING"
– The grip on the barbell.

BEST EVER
The Soviet Union (USSR), China and USA top the medal charts, but special mention to Bulgaria and Poland who also do well. It's Bulgaria's second-best Olympic sport after wrestling.

Pyrros Dimas is the best Olympic weightlifter, with three golds and one bronze, and is Greece's best-ever Olympian. He is nicknamed 'Midas' and began weightlifting at 11.

DIMAS'S MEDAL COUNT: 1 X3 3 X1

CHANCE OF BECOMING A CHAMPION

Slim — OK — Good — Great

Lifting weights is very popular in the gym, but the sport requires different skills and not as many people compete.

UPSIDES
You'll be one of the strongest people in the world, plus you can eat loads of food. Weightlifters sometimes eat 8,000 calories a day — four times the usual amount!

DOWNSIDES
It's painful, repetitive and can make your muscles really sore.

The History Bit
People in prehistoric times used to lift heavy rocks to see who was the strongest and therefore the best. Modern-style weightlifting took off in the 18th and 19th centuries when strongmen performed at the circus. It was so popular it became one of the first modern Olympic sports in 1896, and even included one-handed lifts! Women's weightlifting joined the Olympics in 2000 and powerlifting joined the Paralympics in 1992.

Badminton

WHAT IS IT?

A racket sport where you hit a shuttlecock over a high net. It's very fast and very squeaky.

BASIC TRAINING

Badminton is the perfect garden sport as it's almost impossible to smash a window or ping the shuttlecock into your neighbour's garden. You don't even really need a net to get started, a washing line will do. However, unless one of your family wants to be an umpire, be prepared for loads of arguments . . . "That was in!" . . . "No, it wasn't!" . . . "Yes, it was!" . . . and so on.

RACKET STRINGS
Called catgut, because they used to be made from sheep intestines (not cats' guts!).

VERY LIGHT RACKET
Usually made from carbon fibre.

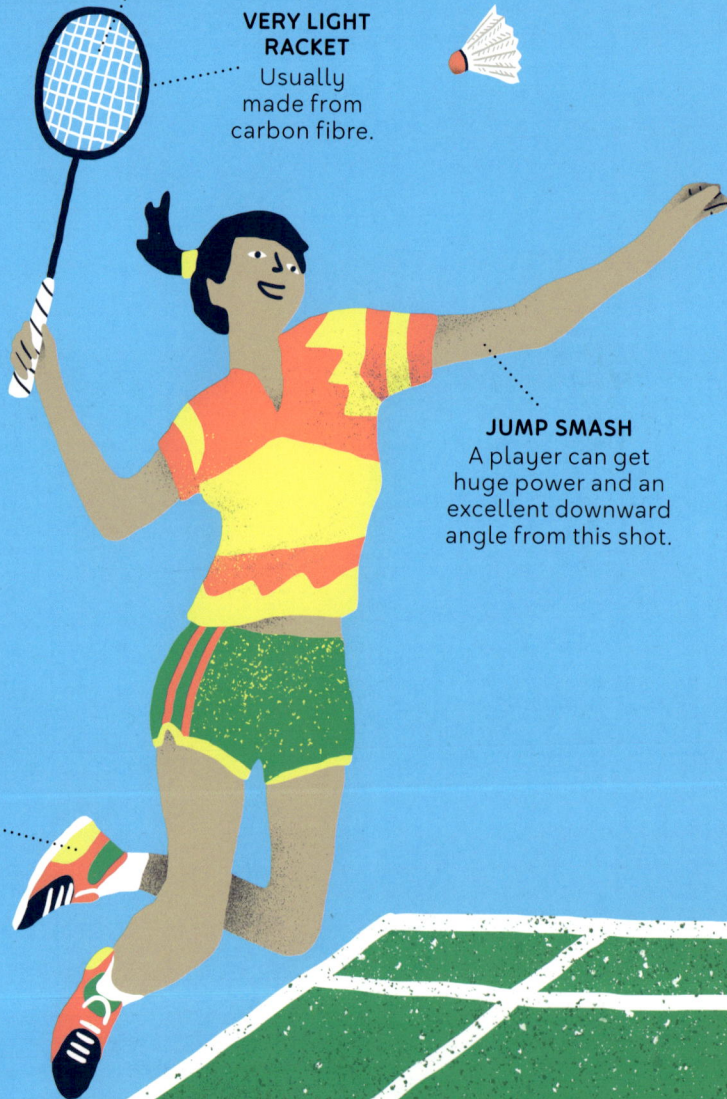

JUMP SMASH
A player can get huge power and an excellent downward angle from this shot.

The History Bit

Originally played in India in the 19th century as *poona*, British soldiers took the game back home, and in 1873 a British duke renamed it after his country house, Badminton. It's lucky the house wasn't called Cow's Bottom. Cow's Bottom . . . or Badminton . . . didn't become an Olympic sport until 1992. It joined the Paralympics in 2021.

SQUEAKIEST TRAINERS YOU'VE EVER HEARD
They sound like a mouse choir when worn inside on a shiny floor.

A CLOSER LOOK

SHUTTLECOCK
Made from 16 overlapping feathers. The fastest recorded speed in a badminton competition is 426 kilometres per hour!

CHANCE OF BECOMING A CHAMPION

Slim ⬆ OK Good Great

It's the second most popular sport worldwide after football, with 220 million players globally. Over a billion people watched the badminton at the Barcelona Olympics in 1992.

SKILLS NEEDED

You will need very bendy wrists as you'll be playing a lot of shots from strange positions.

BEST EVER

China's Gao Ling is the most decorated Olympian. She has four medals, two of them gold. China dominates badminton and has won 41 medals in total, with 20 gold. Indonesia and South Korea are in second and third but they're way behind China.

GAO'S MEDAL COUNT: 🥇 X2 🥈 X1 🥉 X1

UPSIDES

It's the fastest racket sport on Earth, and it's very easy to pick up and play. Smashes are incredibly satisfying too.

DOWNSIDES

People who don't play sometimes think it's a bit of a plinky-plonky game, and the squeaky-shoe-mouse-choir can get a bit annoying.

NET
1.55 metres high, which makes it very hard to jump over if you want to do a fancy victory celebration.

Sound Like a Pro

"PATTY CAKES"
– Where two players hit the shuttlecock back and forth without really moving.

"AIR SHOT"
– When you totally miss the shuttlecock and hit fresh air instead.

"BIRD"
– Another name for the shuttlecock.

"CLEAR"
– A high, deep shot to the back of the court.

"KILL"
– A fast shot that can't be returned.

Epic Fail

At the 2012 Olympics, four women's doubles teams – two South Korean, one Chinese and one Indonesian – were disqualified for losing their matches on purpose. They thought that losing would give them weaker opponents in the next round.

TENNIS

WHAT IS IT?

A racket sport where players try to hit a furry bright-yellow ball over a net using a string-covered circle on a stick.

THE HISTORY BIT

Tennis originally comes from an 11th-century French handball game called *jeu de paume*. Wooden rackets appeared when the rules of modern tennis were invented in 1800, and the game first appeared in the Olympics in 1896. It was dropped after 1924 and returned in 1988, when tennis players had stopped wearing suits and long dresses to play.

TRAINERS AND SHORTS OR A SKIRT AND A TOP
White is the most popular colour.

BALL BOYS AND BALL GIRLS
Teenagers are plucked from local schools to collect all the balls during a match. It's better than doing double maths.

The Rules

Players try to score points by whacking the ball into their opponent's side of the court and hoping it doesn't come back. Tennis can be played by two players (singles) or four players (doubles), and there are also wheelchair events at the Paralympics.

The tennis scoring system has thrown normal counting out of the window. Zero points is called love. The first point you win is 15, the next point is 30 and the next is 40! Then you win the game. If your opponent levels the score at 40–40 it's called deuce, and the next point is called advantage.

The first player to win six games wins a set. The first to win the best of three sets is the winner, except in the men's final, where it's the best of five sets. You might need to play a few times to get the hang of it.

BASIC TRAINING

Let's go back to *jeu de paume* for this bit of basic training. Grab a ball of any size, stand by a wall and throw the ball against it. When the ball comes back, smack it at the wall with the palm of your hand. Keep returning the ball to the wall with your hand until you miss. Just be aware — the wall always wins.

UPSIDES

Top tennis players are some of the most famous and well-paid sports stars in the world. It's a fun workout and there are minimal injuries. You can easily play until you are really old — like 42!

DOWNSIDES

It can be hard to get out of a losing spiral. Losing 6–0, 6–0, 6–0 (known as a triple bagel!) is no fun, however hard you try. Some tennis players lose their temper — with themselves, the umpire and their rackets.

Sound Like a Pro

"ACE"
– A serve so good that your opponent gets nowhere near it.

"GRUNT"
– The noise some players make when hitting a ball.

"SMASH"
– A powerful overhead shot.

"BAGEL"
– A set that ends with the score 6–0.

"SLICE"
– A shot with backspin.

CHANCE OF BECOMING A CHAMPION

Slim	OK		Good	Great

With enough dedication and training, becoming a top player is not as hard as it seems. Lots of parks have free tennis courts to practise on. You just need some balls and a racket.

UMPIRE
Sits in a high chair beside the court. He doesn't wear a bib.

NET
Don't hit the ball into the net or you lose the point. Some players hurdle this when they win.

A CLOSER LOOK

LOTS OF BALLS
You only actually need one, but professional tennis players spend a lot of time studying them, then throwing them away until they find the one they like the look of.

TENNIS BALL
Around 300 million tennis balls are produced each year.

TENNIS RACKET
The most important bit of kit – made from a lightweight metal with strings made from plastic or sometimes animal guts.

INJURIES
Tennis is a very safe sport and most injuries are muscle-related from overstretching or not warming up enough.

SKILLS NEEDED

Players need to be agile and fit to run around a large court, and skilled in different shots, from lobs to backhand returns. A powerful, fast serve is also very handy.

Tennis is a tough mental workout too. The best players can be staring at defeat one minute, then battling back to victory the next.

Finally, you should be able to let out a loud grunt when hitting the ball.

BEST EVER

USA and Great Britain dominate the tennis medal table, with 39 and 43 medals respectively. USA has more golds, with 21.

USA's Venus Williams is the queen of Olympic tennis, with four golds and one silver. Her sister Serena is just behind her, with four golds.

WILLIAMS' MEDAL COUNT: 1 X4   2 X1

Table Tennis

WHAT IS IT?

A bat-and-ball sport that involves hitting a small, light, white ball over a tiny net across a table at ferocious speed.

The Rules

Serve the ball to your opponent's side of the table and hit it back and forth over the net until someone misses or hits it into the net. The first to 11 points, and at least two points clear, wins the game. A match is the best of seven games for singles and the best of five games for doubles.

A CLOSER LOOK

NET
Straight and tight.

CHO
Some players shout "cho" after they've won a good point, to pump themselves up. But too much 'cho-ing' can be considered rude.

BAT
Can also be called a paddle or a racket.

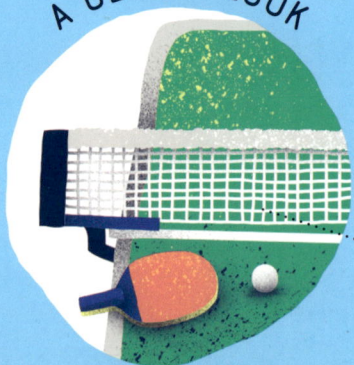

SMALL, PLASTIC BALL
This is white or orange and light as a feather – almost!

UPSIDES

Table tennis smash rallies are some of the most mesmerising things to watch and can go on for ages. The crowd gets louder and louder after every shot.

DOWNSIDES

It's so fast, a really good player can crush you very quickly.

The History Bit

Table tennis was invented in the 1880s by rich Victorians, who wanted an after-dinner game to play on their large dining table. Using books, cigar-box lids and a champagne cork, they created a mini tabletop version of tennis. It was originally called ping-pong, whiff-whaff or flim-flam, and we all know they made a massive error in not sticking with one of those funny names.

Despite its popularity around the world, it took until 1988 for table tennis to make it into the Olympics. However, it's been at the Paralympics since the very start in 1960.

SQUEAKY TRAINERS
Extra-grippy trainers squeak as you make sharp turns and moves.

TABLE TENNIS GRIPS

There are lots of different ways to hold the table tennis bat, but the most common fall into two categories – the shakehand and the penhold, which look exactly like they sound.

Front

Back

Front

Back

SHAKEHAND
Just like shaking someone's hand and also known as the orthodox grip.

PENHOLD
Just like holding a pen, with the handle between thumb and forefinger.

DARK-COLOURED TABLE
So the ball stands out.

Sound Like a Pro

"KILL SHOT"
– A shot that wins the point.

"LOOP"
– An aggressive stroke that generates the most topspin.

"TWO-WINGED LOOPER"
– A player who can play the loop shot well with both forehand and backhand.

"PIMPLES" or **"PIPS"**
– The bobbly side of the table tennis bat, which increases spin on the ball.

"TWIDDLE"
– Twirling your bat around to confuse your opponent about which side of the bat you are going to use.

BASIC TRAINING

Push your kitchen table up against a wall, then fire a ping-pong ball at it and try to return it using the back of a frying pan.

BEST EVER

China dominate table tennis and have won over half of all the medals handed out, with 60 medals, 32 of those gold. The next best is South Korea, with just 18 medals, most of those being bronze.

China have 78 gold out of 129 medals at the Paralympics, but France have more overall medals with 135. Ma Long, nicknamed 'the Dragon', is arguably the greatest table tennis player ever, with five gold medals won across the 2012, 2016 and 2020 Olympics.

MA'S MEDAL COUNT: 🥇 X5

SKILLS NEEDED

You need to be agile and quick on your feet, with great concentration levels and excellent hand–eye coordination. Table tennis is extremely fast – blink and you'll miss it.

CHANCE OF BECOMING A CHAMPION

Slim ↑   OK   Good   Great

Table tennis is one of China's national sports, and children as young as five can be sent to special table tennis schools if they show early talent. To get that gold you'll need to be better than about 300 million Chinese players.

CYCLING

Track

The Rules

There are various short sprints and longer endurance races, including strangely named things like the keirin, pursuit, madison and omnium. They all involve cyclists chasing each other around the 250-metre oval track, trying to cross the winning line first. A keirin involves a person riding a little motorbike in front of the cyclists to set the pace, which looks really strange.

THE HISTORY BIT

Cycling on an indoor track first started in the late 19th century, and it was included in the Olympics in 1896 for men and 1984 for women. It first appeared at the 1996 Paralympics.

WHAT IS IT?

Racing bikes around a large, indoor oval track called a velodrome, while constantly looking over your shoulder to see where everyone else is.

A CLOSER LOOK

HELMET
Special pointy helmets help cyclists cut through the air.

SKIN-TIGHT CLOTHING
With extra padding on the bottom.

TRACK BIKE
These are fast, light and have carbon wheels. They don't bother with brakes or gears.

Road

WHAT IS IT?

A very long bike ride on normal roads to see who is the fastest.

The Rules

Road cycling is very simple – the first to cross the line wins. The race features teams of riders, where teammates work together to help their leader win.

In the time trials, cyclists leave one by one every 90 seconds, but still have to complete the course in the fastest time possible. You are racing the clock.

TEAM JERSEY
With a special pocket on the back to carry tasty food supplies.

The History Bit

Bicycles have been around since the 19th century, but it took inventors a few years to add the pedals and stop making the front wheel massive and the back wheel tiny, aka the penny-farthing. People started racing on bikes with rubber tyres in the 1860s, and road cycling was one of the few sports to be present at the first modern Olympic Games in 1896. It joined the Paralympics in 1984.

GOING FOR A WEE
Cyclists ride for a long time. Some will go behind a tree; some will even go while cycling!

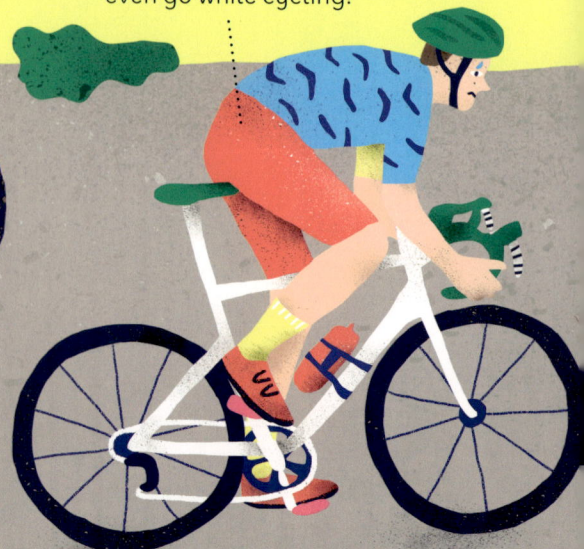

CHANCE OF BECOMING A CHAMPION

Slim	OK	Good	Great

Low. There are limited places in cycling teams and cycling is popular all over the world, so you need to be really good.

Sound Like a Pro

"FIXIE"
– A fixed-gear bike with no brakes.

"DRAFTING"
– When a group of cyclists ride in a line, which helps riders to save energy.

"DROPS"
– Curved part of the handlebars.

"STEED"
– Another name for a bike.

LONG LINE OF RIDERS
When in a team event, cyclists line up behind each other and it can look like a fast train with carriages attached.

SHOES CONNECTED TO THE PEDALS
Cyclists must keep pedalling until the bike slows down and eventually stops.

BEST EVER

Great Britain leads the way in the velodrome with 79 medals, 33 gold. Husband and wife Jason Kenny and Laura Kenny are the most successful male and female cyclists at the Olympics. Jason has seven golds in his nine-medal haul, while Laura has five golds among her six medals. Jason is the most decorated British Olympian of all time.

JASON KENNY'S MEDAL COUNT:
1 x7   2 x2

UPSIDES
You'll get strong legs like tree trunks.

DOWNSIDES
You'll spend most of the time looking at someone else's bottom!

BASIC TRAINING

INJURIES
Some cyclists have gone over the edge of a cliff, but this is very rare.

Put on clothes that are a bit too tight, then sit on the arm of your sofa in a crouched position and pedal your legs round and round for about six hours.

HELMET
Lightweight and full of holes.

Sound Like a Pro

"ATTACK"
– An attempt to pull away from the rest of the cyclists.

"PELOTON"
– The largest group of riders in a race.

"RED LANTERN"
– The cyclist in last place.

"BACON"
– Cuts, scabs, scars and scrapes.

"LID"
– Another name for a helmet.

FINGERLESS GLOVES
To cushion vibrations from the bumpy road.

SKILLS NEEDED
You'll need strong, powerful legs, incredible stamina, strategic thinking and the ability to cycle without toppling over.

SMOOTH LEGS
Riders will shave their legs so it's easier to clean grazes.

ROAD BIKE
Strong but light, with very thin wheels.

85

CYCLING
Mountain Bike

WHAT IS IT?
A long bike race up, down and across lots of different rough terrain like mud, rocks, streams and mountains.

BREATHABLE CLOTHING
You will get sweaty!

PUNCTURE REPAIR KIT
Mountain bikers must do all their own repairs during the race.

MOUNTAIN BIKE
These are lightweight with brakes, suspension and gears.

SHOES
These clip into the pedals to help you generate extra power.

A CLOSER LOOK

FAT TYRES
Thick, knobbly tyres for added grip.

Sound Like a Pro
"GNARLY"
– A difficult part of the course.

"ROOST"
– Dirt kicked up from a sharp turn.

"SNAKE BITE"
– A puncture with two holes next to each other.

"PINNED"
– To go fast.

INJURIES
Going too fast on uneven ground is dangerous and most falls can lead to cuts and bruises, but shoulder, wrist and arm injuries are the most common.

BEST EVER
France's Julien Absalon and Italy's Paola Pezzo have two gold medals each.

ABSALON AND PEZZO'S MEDAL COUNT: 1 X2

The Rules
Around 30–50 riders must ride a number of laps around the cross-country course. It usually takes about an hour and a half to finish, and the first person to cross the finish line wins gold.

THE HISTORY BIT
People started riding their bikes off-road in the 1800s, when they realised that going on a road wasn't always the quickest way. This led to lots of punctures and broken chains, so specialist mountain bikes started being built in the 1970s. Mountain bike racing pedalled its way into the Olympics in 1996.

UPSIDES
You get a really good workout in the great outdoors.

DOWNSIDES
The great outdoors can sometimes bite.

BASIC TRAINING
Find a really dense wood or forest and try to cycle through it.

SKILLS NEEDED
You'll need to enjoy pedalling up hills and getting splattered with mud.

CHANCE OF BECOMING A CHAMPION

Slim		OK	Good	Great

Low. There are only up to 50 places in an Olympic race, so you really need to be one of the best mountain bikers in the world to be picked. Living near a mountain will help.

BMX

WHAT IS IT?

BMX bike racing is done on a bumpy track with lots of obstacles, jumps and tight bends. BMX freestyle is the stunt-riding event, which is full of amazing tricks.

THE HISTORY BIT

BMX started in the USA in the 1960s and was based on a sport called motocross – track racing with motorbikes. It became an official Olympic sport in 2008. Freestyle started in the 1970s and joined the Olympics in 2021.

The Rules

In BMX racing, there's a series of knockout races between sets of eight athletes, until it's whittled down to the final eight racers. Race tracks are usually 300–400 metres long and races last less than a minute. Cross the finish line first to win – simple.

In freestyle, riders take it in turns to do a series of gravity-defying tricks over jumps, ramps, curbs, walls and rails. Judges mark riders on two one-minute runs with a score of 0–100.

CHANCE OF BECOMING A CHAMPION

Slim — OK — Good — Great

Very good. BMX is still a young sport, and your main competitors are teenagers or really old people in their 20s!

A CLOSER LOOK

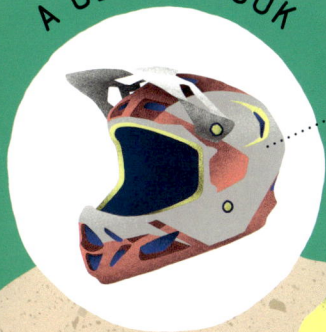

FULL-FACE HELMET
With mouthguard attached.

ELBOW AND KNEE PADS
Built into their clothing.

BMX BIKE
This is a small, lightweight bike with just a back brake.

Sound Like a Pro

"EAT" or "ATE"
– To crash hard or fail terribly.

"BUTCHER"
– A rider who is constantly breaking bits of their BMX.

"BARSPIN"
– Spinning the handlebars round in mid-air and catching them.

"TRUCKDRIVER"
– In mid-air, the rider spins the bike 360 degrees while doing a barspin.

ROLLERS
A set of dirt mounds placed very close together.

INJURIES

The bigger the trick, the nastier the injury.

SKILLS NEEDED

For BMX racing you need to be strong, with powerful legs for pedalling extra fast around the track. Freestylers need a tremendous amount of skill and nerves of steel.

BEST EVER

Latvia's Māris Štrombergs has two golds and a silver in men's BMX racing, while Colombia's Mariana Pajón has two golds and a silver in women's BMX. She's the first Colombian ever to win two golds in any sport and won her first national title aged 5!

ŠTROMBERGS AND PAJÓN'S MEDAL COUNT: 🥇 X2   🥈 X1

UPSIDES

Pulling off an amazing trick looks and feels fantastic.

DOWNSIDES

Crashing or mucking up a big trick.

BASIC TRAINING

Find an empty field and ride as fast as possible towards any muddy hills.

Equestrian

WHAT IS IT?

A jumping and dancing event featuring the only Olympic animal – a horse. Unlike in most other sports, men and women compete against each other.

EVENTING

ALL THE KIT
Riders wear a helmet, breeches, boots, gloves and a body protector so they don't hurt themselves if they fall.

HORSES
Not just any old horse – they need to be bold, careful, athletic and a strong partner with the rider.

WHITE LEG GREASE
In cross-country, some horses have white leg grease to help them slide over the fences.

BASIC TRAINING

Wear your smartest clothes and go and find a huge pile of horse poo to clean up. Try not to get any on your trousers or boots.

INJURIES

If you're unlucky enough to be sent crashing to the ground, you risk broken bones, dislocations and concussions.

The Rules

In jumping, riders complete a course of jumps with lots of twists and sharp turns in the fastest time possible, trying not to get penalised for knocking anything over.

Dressage is the horse ballet one, where horse and rider perform a series of smooth and controlled moves to music. All that's missing are some disco lights. Judges award points for obedience, flexibility and balance, and the highest score wins. Dressage also appears at the Paralympics.

Eventing is three different events on the same horse – dressage, jumping and cross-country. A cross-country course has natural obstacles like fallen trees, walls, water jumps and hedges. The horse and rider with the lowest number of combined penalties win.

THE HISTORY BIT

In the past, humans were very lazy and got bored of walking to places. Luckily, they managed to convince horses to do all the work and even jump over things that got in their way, and so equestrian was born.

The ancient Olympics featured chariot racing, but at the modern Olympics in 1900 they ditched the chariot and stuck to jumping over fences instead.

Skills Needed

You need top-notch horse-riding skills. The rider must use the reins and their legs, shifting their body weight around to communicate with the horse. Talking to the horse isn't allowed but that's OK because nobody really knows how to speak 'horse'.

JUMPING

JUMPING HELMET
Important to protect your noggin if you take a tumble.

FENCE
Horses aren't allowed to knock down any poles, stop in front of a jump or run around it.

UPSIDES
Along with the modern pentathlon, it's the only Olympic sport where you have to control an animal. You can be any age — the second oldest Olympian ever, Austria's Arthur von Pongracz, was 72 when he performed in the 1936 Olympics!

DOWNSIDES
It's dangerous. A horse deciding they have had enough of you on their back or falling on top of you can really hurt. It can get a bit smelly too.

DRESSAGE

DRESSED UP
A tailcoat, white gloves, white breeches, tall black boots and a top hat!

PLAITED MANE
In dressage, the horse needs to look immaculate, with its mane neatly braided.

Sound Like a Pro

"TACK"
— Equipment on a horse, including a saddle and a bridle.

"PIROUETTE"
— The horse turns 360 degrees by turning on the inside back leg.

"NICKER" or **"WHICKER"**
— A horse's soft whinny, used as a greeting to humans or other animals.

"PIAFFE"
— Dressage term for a neat trot on the spot.

"REFUSAL"
— When a horse stops at a jump.

MUSIC
The horse is supposed to dance artfully to the music, so pick your tune wisely. Heavy metal probably wouldn't work!

BEST EVER

Germany leads the pack with 56 medals, 28 gold. Sweden is next with 45 medals, 18 gold.

Germany's Isabell Werth is the most successful Olympic equestrian athlete ever with 12 medals, seven of them gold.

Great Britain has a whopping 64 medals at the Paralympic equestrian, 31 gold. Lee Pearson has 17 medals, 14 gold.

PEARSON'S MEDAL COUNT:
1 X14   2 X2   3 X1

CHANCE OF BECOMING A CHAMPION

| Slim | OK | Good | Great |

Equestrian is not something you can just do in your PE lessons after double maths at school. It is not a cheap sport and riders usually own or have been around horses since they were very young.

SKATEBOARDING

WHAT IS IT?

Riding a small wooden board, with four chunky wheels attached to the bottom, while doing tricks and stunts.

STAIRS
Usually boring things in houses that lead to bedrooms. In skateboarding, you do tricks on them.

SKILLS NEEDED

Balance and courage. Learning all these tricks takes a lot of hard work and some are incredibly dangerous, so if you get them wrong, it really hurts.

THE HISTORY BIT

Skateboarding started in California in the 1950s when surfers decided to take their sport to the streets. It became huge in the 1980s and 1990s, and finally reached the Olympics in 2021.

BASIC TRAINING

Throw yourself on to the concrete playground over and over again – this will help you get used to falling off your board. Falling off is part of skateboarding, so pick yourself up and go again.

A CLOSER LOOK

RAMP
A perfect place to do slash grinds, fakies, blunts, bean plants, staple guns and fly outs. Easy!

SKATEBOARD
The deck is usually made from layers of wood.

The Rules

There are two skate, or SK8 as some people call it, events at the Olympics. 'Street', where riders show off their skills on a street-like course that has stairs, benches, walls, slopes, curbs and angry old men shouting at them (OK, not that bit). Then there's 'park', which has deep and steep bowl-like ramps, which are perfect for performing high mid-air tricks.

Both events are marked by judges, who award points for things like speed, flow, difficulty, originality and probably just for how awesome you are.

CHANCE OF BECOMING A CHAMPION

Slim   OK   Good   Great

If you're still trying to master your first ollie, then you've got a long way to go. Only the cream of the crop will get to the Olympics and, even then, there are only around 80 boarders in total, with a maximum of three from the same country in the same event.

BEST EVER

A new sport at Tokyo 2020, hosts Japan claimed a lot of the glory in the street and park event with three golds, a silver and a bronze in three events. 12-year-old Kokona Hiraki became the youngest Olympic medallist in 85 years when winning silver in the women's park event. However, in the men's park, Australian Keegan Palmer took gold.

INJURIES

There isn't a boarder on earth who hasn't hurt themselves. If you're lucky, it will be a nasty bruise on the shin, some cuts or a bit of road rash. If you're unlucky, you could break a bone, get concussed or lose a tooth . . . or ten.

Sound Like a Pro

"DECK" – The board part of your skateboard.

"STOKED" – Liking something a lot or being really excited.

"SLAM" – A really hard fall.

"NOSE SLIDE" – A slide on the front (nose) of the deck.

"SKETCHY" – Anything that isn't good or trustworthy.

"OLLIE" – Without using their hands, the rider gets their board to do a leap into the air.

TRAINERS
Designed to be comfortable and hard-wearing.

SKATEBOARDER FASHION
Baseball caps, hoodies, T-shirts, baggy jeans or shorts, the list goes on . . .

GRIND RAIL
Riders use all parts of their board to slide along this.

TRUCK
Metal T-shaped pieces that keep the wheels attached.

UPSIDES

There's a great atmosphere at any skate event and the Olympics is no different. Especially as they allow DJs to play music. It's so much fun, the boarders could forget that they're supposed to be battling each other for a gold medal.

DOWNSIDES

Banging your head on the curb after misjudging a trick does not look or feel good. Actually, banging any part of your body anywhere on a concrete surface hurts. If you're a bit of a moaner, then stay away from skateboarding.

QUARTER PIPE
Half a halfpipe – a U-shaped ramp with steep, sloping walls.

WHAT ABOUT THE FUTURE?

New sports are popping up all the time. If enough people in enough countries start to play, and it meets certain criteria set by the people in charge, then one day it too could be at the Olympics. Here are just some sports that could be in the running:

TUG OF WAR

An old-school Olympic event. Two teams try to beat each other by pulling a rope further than their rivals.

Snooker and Billiards

Very smartly dressed players use a stick, or cue, to try and knock different-coloured balls into pockets at the sides and corners of a table covered in green material.

Lacrosse

A sport that was first played by Native Americans. Players use a stick with a net on the end to move the ball between each other and then hopefully score more goals than the other team. Lacrosse was an Olympic sport in the early 1900s.

NETBALL

A team ball sport similar to basketball, but without dribbling or running with the ball. Players are given specific positions and are not allowed to stray outside certain areas of the court. It's arguably faster than basketball because of its three-second passing rule, which also encourages more teamwork.

AIR SPORTS

A wide range of sports that involve being in the air. Everything from drone racing, gliding and parachuting to ballooning, aerobatics and air racing.

CRICKET

Batters try to smash as many runs as they can from a certain number of balls being bowled at them by someone very fast or someone trying to spin it. Lots of strange fielding positions with names like 'square leg' or 'silly mid-on'. Cricket is a massive sport in countries like India and Pakistan, billions of people watch it.

FLAG FOOTBALL

American football is tough, expensive and requires lots of people, so flag football could be more appealing to the Olympics. The sport needs fewer players on a smaller pitch and is not as complicated – a quarterback throws to the receivers and the defence try to stop them. More women and children play flag football than American football, and it could get into the 2028 Olympics in Los Angeles.

CHESS

Two players sit at a table moving pawns, knights, rooks, bishops, queens and kings around a chequered board until someone gets something called 'checkmate'. There's a long set of rules and it can get very complicated, so if you like watching two people silently staring at a board game for hours and hours, then this is the sport for you.

UNDERWATER SPORTS

A wide range of sports that involve being underwater. These include underwater hockey (or octopush), football, rugby, finswimming, freediving, sport diving and aquathlon, which is basically underwater wrestling . . . without the sweat.

Bowling

Hurling a heavy bowling ball down a lane to try and knock over all ten pins to get a 'strike'. Professional bowlers usually get a strike every time they bowl and they also have their own bowling shoes, so they don't have to borrow those stinky ones you get at your local bowling alley.

WUSHU

A Chinese martial art where athletes are judged on their fighting-style routines including kicks, punches and jumps. Some people compare it to gymnastics, but the use of weapons such as swords, spears and nunchucks give it an edge.

FUTSAL

A bit like five-a-side football, but played on a smaller hard-court pitch with a smaller, heavier ball which doesn't bounce very much.

ROLLER SPEED SKATING

This is a high-speed roller-skating race, a bit like speed skating, but done on concrete rather than ice, and with in-line skates rather than ice skates. It's fast, frantic and causes lots of crashes.

POLO

Having first appeared at the Olympics in 1900, one of the oldest sports could make a comeback. Teams of four polo players ride horses, which they call ponies, and try to score goals by hitting a small, hard ball through the rival team's goal using a long-handled mallet.

KARTING

Pushing to become the first motorsport at the Olympics. Drivers race their electric karts around a track. Unlike in most professional motorsports, the karts are all the same, so it's a true test of the driver's skill.

ACROBATIC GYMNASTICS

A bit like very complicated cheerleading. Groups of gymnasts perform elegant spins, twists, dances and tumbles to music. It involves a high level of technical choreography and skill, as well as trust.

Squash

This is a very fast racket sport where players thwack a small, squidgy ball against some walls until their opponent can't hit it back any more.

SUMO

An ancient Japanese type of wrestling where two large men, wearing massive loincloths called *mawashi*, try and push each other outside of a ring. Sumo is loaded with tradition and wrestlers have a very strict way of life and training.

ULTIMATE FRISBEE

A mixed-team sport where players score points by passing a plastic disc to a teammate in the opposing team's end zone. It's a million miles away from chucking the Frisbee about on the beach for your dog to catch.

Glossary

APPARATUS — The equipment artistic gymnasts use.

ATHLETE — A person who is good at sport — usually they are very fit and talented.

ATTACKER — A player in a team who tries to score goals or points.

BATON — A short metal rod that athletes quickly hand to each other during a relay race.

BOUT — The name for a match or a period of time in a combat sport.

BULLSEYE — The centre of a target.

BUNKER — A big sandpit that traps golf balls.

CARBON FIBRE — A strong, lightweight material made from carbon.

CHALK — The white powder athletes use on their hands to help with their grip.

CONCUSSION — When a whack on the head makes you all wobbly or you pass out.

DEBUT — The first appearance.

DEFENDER — A player who tries to stop the attacking players on the other team from scoring.

DISQUALIFICATION — No more sport for you — bye-bye!

DRIBBLE — When a player moves the ball in a certain direction — it doesn't involve saliva.

FIBREGLASS — A lightweight material made from fine glass fibres.

FLEET — A group of boats sailing together.

FOUL — An unfair move or play in sport.

GOALKEEPER or **GOALIE** — A player who protects the goal.

HALFPIPE — A U-shaped ramp used to perform skateboarding tricks.

HORSE — A gymnastic apparatus and the only Olympic animal.

INJURY — Something that usually hurts and may mean you can't compete any more.

JUDGE — A person who awards marks or points in artistic or combat sports.

KNOCKOUT — When a boxer punches their opponent to the ground and their opponent can't get up again.

MARATHON — A very long race, around 42 kilometres (26.2 miles).

MAT — A soft floor covering that helps prevent athletes hurting themselves when they land on it.

MEDAL — A disc of gold, silver or bronze that is hung around an athlete's neck if they come first, second or third.

MIDDLE AGES — A long time ago when people didn't have the Internet.

NET — Strung between goalposts to stop a ball or across a court or table to provide a barrier in racket sports.

OAR — A stick used to paddle a boat or canoe.

OLYMPIC FLAME — A big torch that burns in the Olympic stadium during the Games.

OLYMPIC GAMES — If you don't know about these by now, you haven't been paying attention.

OPPOSITION or **OPPONENT** — The rival for your medal.

OUTFIELD PLAYER — Any player who's not a goalkeeper.

PARALYMPIC GAMES — You really haven't been paying attention, have you?

PENALTY — A foul or mistake, usually resulting in a shot at a goal or points being deducted.

POOL — A large rectangle of water where swimmers compete.

PROFESSIONAL — Someone who gets paid to do a job.

PROSTHESES — Artificial body parts.

RACKET — A round bat with strings used in tennis and badminton.

RALLY — A lot of back-and-forth shots in a court game, like tennis, badminton or volleyball. A rally ends when a player fails to hit it back.

REFEREE — An official who keeps an eye on the rules and stops people cheating.

RELAY — A race where each stage is run by a different member of the team.

SAIL — A big, triangle-shaped piece of material that helps power a boat.

SECOND WORLD WAR — A war that took place between 1939 and 1945.

SINGLET — A vest.

SPECTATOR — A person watching a sport, either live or on television.

STAMINA — The energy inside you that keeps you going.

STONE AGE — Even longer ago than the Middle Ages.

SUBSTITUTE — A player who replaces another player when they are tired or playing badly.

TACTICS — Special plans that help a team or an individual to reach their goal.

TORCH RELAY — The Olympic flame is passed around the country before being taken to the Olympic stadium to start the Games.

TOURNAMENT — A big sporting event with a lot of athletes or teams.

TRACK — An oval-shaped running area where athletes perform.

UMPIRE — Another word for a referee.

VICTORY — A win.

VICTORY PODIUM — The special platform that an athlete stands on to receive their medal.

VISUALLY IMPAIRED — Someone who is blind or partially blind.

WEIGHT CATEGORY — In many sports, athletes are weighed and placed in an appropriate group.

INDEX